Devoted

38 EXTRAORDINARY TALES
OF LOVE, LOYALTY, AND LIFE WITH DOGS

◆ REBECCA ASCHER-WALSH ◆

**NATIONAL
GEOGRAPHIC**

WASHINGTON, D.C.

OPPOSITE: *Wilma and her owner, Steve Sietos, a New York City fireman*

CONTENTS

Love, Honor, & Devotion

◆ REBECCA ASCHER-WALSH ◆

My first wedding was a low-key affair. My grandmother made my dress out of white curtains. My mother was the sole witness as I vowed until death do us part. Sadly, my groom and I would have only ten years together, but such are the risks a six-year-old takes marrying her beloved golden retriever. ◆ I eventually married a member of my own species. But throughout my life a dog or two has been beside me, offering love at every turn regardless of how sharp those turns might be. Among my past beloveds are a bullmastiff and a standard poodle. Now, I volunteer at a crowded city shelter where the majority of dogs are pit bulls and the euthanasia rate is high. I founded a not-for-profit that provides financial assistance for those pits lucky enough to be rescued, because my heart beats fastest for this misunderstood breed whose loyalty, intelligence, and kindness are unparalleled. My own two pit bulls are my children's steadfast companions, ridden like horses by day before settling in to keep watch by their beds at night. Such is their devotion.

And such is the devotion of the dogs in this book. Whether they have proved themselves through single acts of heroism or lifetimes of loyalty, they are exceptional. But perhaps their greatest legacy is the ability to restore our faith in the existence of unconditional love. Through their unique stories, the dog owners in this book reminded me to express my gratitude to the ever present examples of devotion sitting by my side. I rescued them, but they have rescued me in return. Dogs make our hearts grow larger. Such is their magic. And such is the magic of these stories. ◆

OPPOSITE: *Author Rebecca Ascher-Walsh and her two rescue pit bulls, Desiree (left) and Buddy (right)*

Cheyenne

AMERICAN STAFFORDSHIRE TERRIER ◆ GEORGIA

David E. Sharpe, a senior airman in the United States Air Force, returned from his deployment to Saudi Arabia in 2002. It was a joyless homecoming: Suffering residual trauma from his deployment, he drank too much, picked fights, and punched holes in the refrigerator door. A friend suggested that he get a dog, so he adopted a brown-and-white pit bull puppy named Cheyenne. ◆ Three months later, "Things got really bad,"

Sharpe remembers. "I had two military buddies who committed suicide, and I couldn't deal with what was in my head. I went to my room and took out a .45 my father had given me that he had in Ranger school. I was crying and calling myself a loser, and then I pulled the hammer back, put the barrel in my mouth and my thumb on the trigger. And as soon as I did that, one of the weirdest things happened. This little pup, who was maybe six months old at the time, came up and licked my ear, which distracted me so I took the gun out of my mouth to ask, 'What did you do that for?' And then she came over and sat down in my lap and put her head on my right thigh. The pistol was on my left. I understood it was an ultimatum to choose her or to take my life. I chose her, and I never looked back."

PETE the pup from the original *Little Rascals* was a pit bull.

OPPOSITE: *Cheyenne and her owner, David Sharpe, share a hug.*

AMERICAN STAFFORDSHIRE TERRIER

- ◆ ORIGIN: **England**
- ◆ COLOR(S): **Any color**
- ◆ HEIGHT: **17 to 19 inches**
- ◆ TEMPERAMENT: **The American Staffordshire terrier (aka Pit Bull) is a people-pleasing, family dog that flourishes when given a job or activity.**

In 2009, Sharpe founded Companions for Heroes (formerly Pets2Vets), which pairs veterans, active duty military personnel, emergency first responders, and their families with rescue dogs; the organization pays the adoption fee and offers free veterinary care for a year as well as unlimited access to a trainer. Sharpe, who now works in counterintelligence, says the pairing of a dog and a veteran is the beginning of returning that person to active society. "They choose the dog themselves from the shelter, and if it works out well—and we have a 98 percent success rate—they have made a good choice. Then they learn how to train their dog, and they are empowered by that. And then they start making other choices—to

go back to school, to take advantage of the GI Bill, to get a job."

One veteran who has benefited is Lance Cpl. Jason Allen, a U.S. Marine Corps sniper who did tours in Africa, South America, and the Middle East. His last tour was in Afghanistan, where he ran over a roadside bomb. Allen survived, but back home in Texas he was immobilized by pain. He dropped from 150 pounds to 115. He lived his days in despair and suffered flashbacks at night. Desperate, he sat down with a loaded gun, planning to commit suicide.

His wife talked him out of his suicide attempt and Allen spent three days under observation at the veterans hospital, but when he returned home he was no better. Then, channel surfing one evening, he saw a television segment on Companions for Heroes. "We were talking about . . . getting radical shock therapy at that point, and I said to my wife, 'Let's give this a try instead.' " With the organization's approval, the couple went to the shelter and adopted Sarge, a Boston terrier mix. Within days, the dog had changed Allen's life.

"I had been told by the doctor that I should give up physical activity because they couldn't manage my pain," he says, "but when we got

Sharpe, a war veteran, found salvation in saving a pit bull named Cheyenne.

Sarge, it's not like you can't play with this dog. And he needs to be walked, so we walk. Sarge has given me a new purpose. He's not a good dog, he's a great dog." When Allen is awakened by a flashback, Sarge pads outside after him; Allen says he now returns to bed in ten minutes, rather than the 90 it took to quiet himself before Sarge.

Sarge's ability to read his master's moods doesn't surprise Julie Hecht, a canine behavioral researcher in Professor Alexandra Horowitz's Dog Cognition Lab at Barnard College. "Someone having a flashback will have a physiological change that a dog will definitely pick up on," she says, "and what's interesting is that for many dogs, it's a natural response to be calm and close, so it sets a scene in which the dog can slide into its natural state." Hecht points out that comforting a human during such an episode is mutually beneficial; the person is quieted, and the dog is generally rewarded by affectionate petting.

Sharpe's dream is that every veteran would arrive stateside and head to the nearest shelter.

Cheyenne inspired Sharpe to start the organization Companions for Heroes, pairing veterans with pets.

"Eighteen vets kills themselves a day [in the United States]. That's over 6,000 a year. I want that number to be zero," he says. "And every eight seconds a [shelter] animal is euthanized. I want that number reduced. I remember being in bed with Cheyenne and crying to her about my nightmares," he continues. "I would say to her, 'I'm going crazy. How am I going to live? How am I ever going to have a wife?' And here Cheyenne and I are, 12 years later, and my wife and I just had a son. The thing about having a dog is you're not a disabled dog owner. You're just a dog owner. And they are there with complete and unconditional love." ◆

WHAT MAKES DOGS SUCH GOOD THERAPY? Though scientific evidence is limited, vast anecdotal evidence strongly suggests that pets have incredibly positive effects on those suffering from PTSD and/or depression. Interactions between dogs and their owners have shown to increase levels of the "feel-good" hormone, oxytocin.

Ricochet

GOLDEN RETRIEVER ◆ CALIFORNIA

Petulance is underrated. For Ricochet, it was the very quality necessary to find her calling. Ricochet was bred and raised to be a service dog, and for the first four months of her life, the golden retriever did as asked. She opened the fridge; she turned on the lights; she was "brilliant and enthusiastic," remembers her owner, Judy Fridono. And then, she staged a sit-in. "She would just walk away from training sessions and lie down. I tried to remotivate her because I knew she was smart, but she just wasn't interested in anything, except chasing birds. She seemed to have no work ethic. Her littermates were excelling and I couldn't figure her out. I took her to doctors, I took her to chiropractors, I took her to animal communicators to try to figure out what was wrong with this dog. It wasn't a happy time."

There was only one thing that Ricochet seemed to enjoy, and that was balancing on a surfboard in a kiddie pool, an activity used to help hone service dogs' coordination. So when Fridono heard about a dog surfing competition near their home in California, she entered it as a Hail Mary. "It was definitely a love-hate relationship with Ricochet at that point for me," says Fridono, "but I thought this might be fun for her. I figured she'd surf a

GOLDEN RETRIEVERS are one of the most popular breeds in the United States.

GOLDEN RETRIEVER

* ORIGIN: **Scottish Highlands**
* COLOR(S): **Rich, radiant golden of various shades**
* HEIGHT: **21.5 to 24 inches**
* TEMPERAMENT: **Golden retrievers are friendly, active, and energetic. While they can adapt to many different living situations, they require daily exercise.**

couple of waves and she'd be done." Instead, Ricochet won third place. "I was brought to tears," her owner remembers. "It was the first time after all those months she was really good at something. "

Fridono was determined to find a way for Ricochet to give back with her newfound skill. "I don't believe in breeding dogs to breed, because there are so many homeless animals, and I felt that I had brought this dog into the world so she had to do something meaningful." So Fridono decided that the dog could help raise money for charity, and reached out to an acquaintance, Patrick Ivison. Ivison, a high school student and

a surfer, had been in an accident that left him quadriplegic at the age of 14 months. The two planned an event where the boy and dog would surf side by side to help pay for Ivison's physical therapy.

"I was totally stoked to meet her," remembers Ivison. "And I loved the idea of catching a party wave." But Ricochet had a different idea. On one of the first rides, "she jumped off the board and onto my back. You could see everyone had the same thought at the same time: 'Let's try this on purpose.' So we got a bigger board, put her on the back, and pushed me into a wave," says Ivison. "And it worked perfectly." Adds Fridono, "Here was a dog who had never wanted to do anything, and she never wanted to stop. She was reborn that day."

Ivison's outing with Ricochet raised $10,000 and also helped him earn a grant to pay for three years of his physical therapy. "I remember saying to Patrick's mom, 'How are we ever going to top this?'" says Fridono. "Little did I know this was just the beginning."

OPPOSITE: *Patrick Ivison and Ricochet share a board and a wave.*

Ivison, Ricochet, and supporters enjoy the waves at Cardiff State Beach in San Diego, California.

In less than two years, Ricochet has helped to raise ten times that amount for various charities through online campaigns, inspiring contributions by surfing both solo and tandem. Among those she has shared a board with are a woman whose leg is amputated at the pelvis and another with no arms. Both women rely on Ricochet to help them balance on the board, as does Ivison. "I generally fall off on purpose at the end of a wave to avoid getting hurt, but she balances the board so I don't have to," he says. "We ride all the way to shore." "No matter what, she adjusts to each person's disability," says Fridono, "whether it's by standing on the front of the board, or the back, or standing sideways. I don't know how she does it."

That's an innate gift that comes with having four legs, a low center of gravity, and the lack of awareness that a big wave can really mess you up, says canine expert and trainer Philip Levine. "Dogs are quadrupeds and acutely aware of their position on the earth at all times," he explains. "What could be more imperative to an animal than your footing?" As anyone who has tried leash training a stubborn dog by pulling back can attest, "They will instinctively correct their balance in an opposition reflex," says Levine, who suggests a tug sideways instead. On a surfboard, when it comes to riding a wave without embellished movement, says Levine, "a dog would be pretty hard to beat."

But to those who have become familiar with Ricochet—her video on YouTube has been viewed by more than four million people—her gift is nothing less than magical. "She inspired me to have hope," says Ivison, who now considers Ricochet a member of the family. "And I get emails from all over the world from people saying they were desperate until they saw us and we gave them the hope to keep going." What touches people the most, he says, is that "we are both comeback stories. Ricochet was supposed to be a service dog, but instead of serving just one family she has gotten to help millions."

Her owner is now one of her biggest fans. Says Fridono, "I really struggled with her, but this is what she chose. She took a different journey than I thought she would, but looking back on it, it all makes perfect sense. None of this would have happened if I hadn't let her be who she needed to be." ◆

> " Here was a dog who had never wanted to do **anything,** and she never wanted to stop. She was reborn that day."

WHY IS RICOCHET SUCH A NATURAL SURFER? Originally trained in the late 1800s to retrieve waterfowl during a hunt, golden retrievers have had an instinctive love of water for generations. They're physically adapted as well—a dense inner coat provides warmth while a water-repellent outer coat helps them dry quickly.

DeeDee

GREYHOUND ◆ IOWA

When Brooke Lim adopted DeeDee, a two-year-old retired racing greyhound, it was with the intention of training her to comfort people who were ailing. Never could Lim have dreamed that she would be the patient for whom DeeDee would ultimately care. ◆ "I wanted to have a job with my dog that would make people's lives better," she explains of her decision to have DeeDee certified as a therapy dog, which allows the animals into public areas after proper permission is obtained, to provide comfort. "Greyhounds are perfect at it because they have a calm demeanor, they have soulful eyes that melt your heart, and they are the right height for people to be able to reach." Within a year, DeeDee had completed the testing and she and her owner were regulars at local hospices and nursing homes.

Then Lim was diagnosed with the neurological disease myalgic encephalomyelitis, which can cause muscle pain, weakness, and loss of balance. "It was like I was sick with the flu all the time," says Lim, who lives in Ottumwa, Iowa. "I started not to have the ability to go out, and as I began to do less, I could see that DeeDee really needed a

> **GREYHOUNDS** were bred as hunting dogs because of their capacity to see small animals across great distances and their ability to quickly reach high speeds.

OPPOSITE: *DeeDee, a retired greyhound, takes a break from her service to rest on her new bed.*

DeeDee with her owner, Brooke Lim, in their backyard

job." And so Lim began teaching DeeDee to be a service dog—her service dog—who would be able to accompany her freely into public areas to help Lim.

Lim started by training DeeDee to retrieve, something greyhounds (unlike dogs like golden or Labrador retrievers) don't generally do spontaneously. "I made it fun for her by putting peanut butter in an empty container. You work with what the dog has. The finished product of a service dog can look so fancy, but it's about common sense." Soon,

- Greyhounds are among the fastest dogs, reaching speeds of 43 miles an hour.
- On October 7, 2006, a greyhound named Cinderella May a Holly Grey set a new world record for the canine high jump: 68 inches.
- Greyhounds have the highest red blood cell count of any dog. Red blood cells carry oxygen throughout the body, so greyhounds' high count most likely contributes to their speed.

Lim had trained DeeDee to pick things up that she dropped, to help with the laundry, to pull her out of bed, and then to pull the covers up over the bed to make it.

Lim soon discovered that DeeDee would naturally alert her if she began to lose her balance. "The amazing thing is that she has trained herself to know when I'm about to have a total loss of balance, even when I don't even sense it," says Lim. "She will cross in front of me and put her head down and look away from me, so I know. And when I fall, I can put my arms around her and she will brace me."

Canine expert and teacher Philip Levine says that because greyhounds have been bred in part for their sight, they are extremely sensitive to visual cues, making it possible for DeeDee to be aware of Lim's smallest motions. "It wouldn't surprise me if she was attuned to any irregularities of head movement, eye movement, and fluidity of movement," he explains of DeeDee's ability to sense an oncoming collapse in her owner. "In addition, greyhounds are extremely sensitive animals, more so than most."

Their teamwork, says Lim, suits them both. "DeeDee has a purpose," she says, "And I no longer feel complete without her. I literally put my life in her paws, and she comes through for me again and again." ◆

RETIRED GREYHOUND RACERS Greyhounds bred for racing are usually removed from the racing circuit if they do not win or place in a few consecutive races. In the past, losing dogs were often put to sleep. Today many greyhound rescue organizations promote the adoption of racing greyhounds. Up to 20,000 greyhounds are adopted yearly.

Schoep

MIXED BREED ◆ WISCONSIN

John Unger and his then fiancée spent 18 months canvassing Wisconsin shelters, looking for the perfect dog. When they saw a German shepherd mix cowering in the corner of his kennel with his back to the door, they recognized him as the pet of their dreams. "We wanted to work with an abused dog," Unger explains, "and to bring out his full potential. To help a dog who was completely unsocialized learn how to be a *dog*, free and easy and without fear."

They certainly had their work cut out for them. Schoep, named for the famous Wisconsin ice cream, had grown up in the wild, being fed by a friendly stranger until he was brought into the shelter. He appeared never to have seen a leash or a ball, and he was terrified of men. "The first night he didn't sleep at all so I stayed awake with him, lying down on the floor in front of him without approaching him, so he could begin to process that I was there and wasn't going to hurt him," says Unger. For the first few months, "I always made sure to walk in front of him, so he could keep me in his sight line. And I would massage him or lightly touch him." Soon, Schoep was responding with kisses. "He started to

DOGGIE "ICE CREAM" is a nondairy frozen treat packed with protein, vitamins, and minerals. It comes in flavors such as vanilla and peanut butter.

OPPOSITE: *Schoep and his owner, John Unger, enjoy a moment in Lake Superior.*

- Rin Tin Tin, the first dog movie star, appeared on the screen in 1922 and went on to make a total of 26 films.
- Berry starred in the Harry Potter film series as Sirius Black's "animagus" form, a black dog, who would watch over Harry from the shadows and protect him.
- Rando, a canine actor, had a starring role in the 1989 comedy *K-9* about a detective and his drug-sniffing and chaos-producing furry partner, Jerry Lee.

sit on my foot with his back to me," remembers Unger, "wanting his back rubbed. I had earned his trust."

Two years later, in 1998, Unger and his fiancée had broken up (they shared custody of Schoep until she moved out of state), and Unger was feeling suicidal. One January night, he walked the dog down to the lake intending to drown himself. "I can't understand why I would have brought him and put him in that position even now, but I'm so glad I did," says Unger. "I was crying and about to do it and he looked up at me with a look I've never seen before or since, with a kind of furrow in his brow like a person would have if they were confused. And I immediately snapped out of that place of despair. I was only thinking of him then, and how I had almost left him alone. We spent the night walking the streets, and then went to bed. And when I woke up the next afternoon, I felt entirely different. He really did save me."

From that moment on, Unger took Schoep to the lake purely for relaxation. "He doesn't know how to swim, so I used to hold him in my arms, and one day, he just fell asleep, " says Unger. "Now he falls asleep almost instantly." Hard of hearing, with failing vision, and suffering from arthritis, the dog's aching joints are soothed by the waters of Lake Superior, where they go now to "swim," and his owner relishes the time spent cradling Schoep.

One such moment was captured by Unger's friend the photographer Hannah Stonehouse Hudson; when she posted the photo to her Facebook account, the image became a viral

Schoep and Unger visit the lake to relax and to ease Schoep's arthritis.

sensation. "I think in today's world we are faced with such heaviness, we are moving too fast, and people look at this photograph and say, 'That's the way the world should be, filled with compassion, love and hope,' " says Unger. "People are just longing for it. And that's the way I feel about Schoep. We understand each other, we are compassionate towards each other, and we love each other. He is my world." ◆

HOW CAN YOU TREAT YOUR DOG'S ARTHRITIS? One out of every five adult dogs suffers from arthritis. Beyond medication, special orthopedic dog beds and upholstered steps that help your dog climb up on the sofa (rather than jump) can ease your dog's joint pain.

Doogie

People go to amazing lengths to show devotion to their dogs, whether by preparing home-cooked meals, giving up their favorite spot on the couch, or…wrestling a threatening alligator. ◆ Gary Murphy, a 72-year-old from Palm City, Florida, has upped the ante for what it means to be a protective dog owner. One morning, as he was working on his boat docked in the river behind his backyard, Murphy saw his 11-year-old West Highland white terrier, Doogie, go into the water alongside the dock to cool his feet. And then he heard a yelp. "I looked down and a gator had him in his mouth and was taking him into the water. I jumped ten feet over the rail off the dock and landed on top of the gator so he would let the dog go, and then I grabbed his nose and tried to punch him on the soft spot. I've been watching too many *Swamp People* episodes."

The gator reared up, throwing Murphy off and swimming away. Murphy spent the next ten hours cleaning the dog's wounds and cradling him in a towel. It was only at midnight that Murphy began to shake with fear, and it had nothing to do with the trauma of the fight with the alligator. "I just started shaking realizing I

OFFICIALS ESTIMATE that more than a million alligators can be found in the state of Florida.

OPPOSITE: *Doogie enjoys climbing the trees on Boy Scout Island along Florida's Intracoastal Waterway.*

WEST HIGHLAND WHITE TERRIER

- ORIGIN: **Scotland**
- COLOR(S): **White**
- HEIGHT: **10 to 11 inches**
- TEMPERAMENT:
  Spunky, devoted, friendly, alert, and courageous. Westies make great family pets.

had almost lost him. We are together all the time. He sleeps with his head on my pillow at night. He's my shadow and I'm his alpha dog."

Doogie, whom Murphy and his wife, Linda, had adopted from a shelter six years earlier, spent the next few days recuperating at the vet. He was released with some bruising, but the vet assured the Murphys he would be just fine. Three weeks later, however, the gator—which was more than 8 feet long and weighed 320 pounds—returned, lounging in the mangroves by the dock.

Murphy called the wildlife agency; it sent a team to fetch the alligator, which they later proclaimed to be, says Murphy, "the most aggressive gator they had ever caught."

Murphy and Doogie quickly returned to their happy routines; Murphy works on his boat while Doogie digs holes and hunts snakes. "He's the smartest dog I've ever met," says Murphy. "I wish my children were this smart." He adds that he's no more afraid of alligators than he ever was ("They were here long before I was—it takes a long time to get that ugly—and they don't generally bother us"), and explains that because of the construction of a bridge up the river, the creatures' natural habitat had been disturbed that particular month. Still, "I would do it all over again," he says. "I'm nuts. And I don't know what I would ever do if I lost my dog." ◆

WHY DO WESTIES HAVE WHITE COATS? When the breed was first being established in Scotland, the breed came in a variety of colors including black, red, cream, and white. Legend has it, while out on a hunt one day a red Westie was confused with a fox and mistakenly shot. From then on, the predominant Westie breeder encouraged white-coated dogs.

Hooch

MIXED BREED ◆ AUSTRALIA

From the first day that Sean Herbert, an Australian aviation company owner, adopted Hooch from a pound, the two were inseparable. So when the Cavalier King Charles spaniel–blue heeler cross came racing up the tarmac after him as Herbert was preparing to go skydiving, he took it in stride. "The person by the door of the plane grabbed the dog and said, 'Is this yours?' just as we were taking off," he recalls. "The pilot wasn't about to look after a puppy, so I duct-taped her to the inside of my suit, and we jumped. She seemed pretty happy." Soon, thanks to a specially designed harness, Hooch was making weekly tandem jumps with her owner.

Hooch also insisted on riding on Herbert's motorcycle and Jet Ski, and when he went scuba diving, she would jump overboard and attempt to dive down after him. Ever the thoughtful owner, Herbert went to work designing scuba gear for Hooch. At a lighting store, he found an item that became a frame for her mask. "The store owner wasn't happy that I was trying light shades on my dog, but when I explained what I was trying to do, he was very helpful," Herbert

SOME 14,000 YEARS of companionship between man and dog have helped man's best friend develop remarkable abilities to understand humans and their behaviors.

PAGE 31: *Hooch and her owner, Sean Herbert, parachute from 12,000 feet near Sydney, Australia.*

- Tillman: This stocky bulldog holds a Guinness World Record as the fastest skateboarding dog, covering 100 meters in 19.678 seconds. Tillman also enjoys snowboarding, surfing, and skimboarding.
- Part-Ex: This Jack Russell from the UK has been taking part in extreme sports since he was 18 months old. Some of his favorites include kayaking, rock jumping, wind surfing, and coasteering.

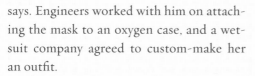

Hooch made 14 scuba dives and 53 parachute jumps.

says. Engineers worked with him on attaching the mask to an oxygen case, and a wetsuit company agreed to custom-make her an outfit.

Before long, the pair started training—first in a pool, then in the shallows, and eventually graduating to reef diving. "She would get to the bottom and walk away from me, exploring things around her," Herbert remembers. "She was very interested in what was going on."

Hooch, who made 14 dives before being forced to retire after she broke her leg falling out of bed, inherited a genetic fault from her Cavalier King Charles lineage that, explains Herbert, "[causes] their hearts to grow too big for their bodies." She died from cardiac arrest at the age of 15, having seen more of the world than many of us could ever hope to. ◆

GOING TO EXTREMES ON THE SILVER SCREEN We all know stuntpeople take the fall for their human counterparts, but what about the dogs? One of the most famous dogs of the silver screen, Rin Tin Tin, first appeared in silent films of the 1920s . . . doing his own stunts.

Hank

GREAT DANE ◆ MISSOURI

When McKenzie, who lives in Kansas City, Missouri, was brutally attacked by her boyfriend during an argument, her Great Dane, Hank, risked his well-being to protect her: Shielding McKenzie with his body, the dog took the brunt of the assault, suffering two broken ribs and a fractured hip. Hours later, when McKenzie was offered a bed at the Rose Brooks Center, a domestic violence shelter, she returned the favor.

On the telephone from the police station, with nowhere else to go, McKenzie told the person on the hotline, "I'm not coming without my dog."

"The shelter said, 'We don't take dogs,' " McKenzie remembers. "And I said, 'We aren't separating.' " Concerned for her well-being, the shelter—with space for a hundred abused women and their children—agreed to put both up for the night. "We figured it was a one-day thing," says the center's spokesperson, Sarah North, "and we'd do whatever we had to in order to make it work."

As a quick fix, the staff turned a bathroom into a kennel for Hank, having no idea that the shelter would be home for the next three months while the two healed. They ended up

THE WORLD'S TALLEST DOG is a Great Dane named Zeus. This tall pup stands 44 inches tall and was three years old at the time of the record.

OPPOSITE: *Hank, a Great Dane, helped protect his owner during a domestic violence attack.*

GREAT DANE

- ORIGIN: **Germany**
- COLOR(S): **Brindle, fawn, blue, black, harlequin, and mantle**
- HEIGHT: **28 to 32 inches**
- TEMPERAMENT: **Popular family pets, great Danes are courageous, friendly, and dependable.**

changing the course of the institution forever.

"We had always known the benefits of having animals for the families," says North. "Children are incredibly resilient about leaving their houses, their schools, their fathers. But the leaving of the pet can be the breaking point." For many abused women, leaving the pet isn't an option, and that means they stay in abusive situations. "One study said that 82 percent of women in shelters reported that their abuser had also either abused their animals or threatened to kill them," says North. "Up to 40 percent of women say they [would] have left their abuser earlier if they could have brought their pets. But we were in the children-and-women business, not the dog business."

When the media began to spread the story of McKenzie and Hank, donations started pouring in from across the world. Empowered by the experience with Hank—who, North says, had a therapeutic effect on staff members as well as on residents—shelter management made a plan. In June 2012, the Rose Brooks Center became the first shelter in the United States to have an on-site kennel—which houses as many as eight dogs and cats belonging to visiting families—and one of only a few to offer any kind of housing to families' animals. "This was a dream of mine," says McKenzie. "When I came into the shelter, I said, 'I don't want to be the last woman who brings her dog with her.'"

The benefits extend beyond enabling families to leave abusive situations and remain intact as a clan. According to North, the dog's presence can supply the first step in healing a family in which the mother is emotionally shut down from trauma. "Pets can offer a bridge for rebuilding the family unit and reconnecting them," she says. "It can be as simple as the fact that every night, the family can take the dog for a walk around the block together, and begin to talk."

Hank and his owner, McKenzie, make an appearance at Cabaret, an event benefiting the Rose Brooks Center.

As for McKenzie and Hank, they are now living happily in their own apartment and getting on with their lives. "There was never a reason to protect me before, but he's pretty protective now," she says of her pet. With any perceived threat, "he will position himself so he's crossed in front of me, between me and that person." McKenzie now feels entirely secure in the world again, thanks to her dog. "I feel safe knowing he's safe," she says. "My goal now is to serve him. My goal is that he should not have to do anything for me, ever, ever again." ◆

HOW DOGS CAN HELP HEAL Dogs are known to be excellent stress relievers. Petting a dog can calm you down and lower blood pressure. It causes your brain to release endorphins, which buffer the negative effects of stress.

Shana

MIXED BREED ◆ NEW YORK

S hana, who is half wolf and half German shepherd, wasn't born to be wild. But when her owners' lives were threatened, her feral survival instincts and ingenuity saved the day. ◆ Part of a litter bred illegally to fight pit bulls, Shana was rescued from her fate by a family, only to be surrendered to a local shelter for euthanasia when the family discovered New York State requires a license to house a wolf. Instead of killing Shana,

the shelter contacted Eve and Norman Fertig, who ran the Enchanted Wildlife Sanctuary in nearby Alden, New York. "She had fleas, she had worms, oh, she was a mess," remembers Eve. "But I got her the best care, and she turned out to be the gentlest animal I have ever met." Her wolf heritage does shine through in one respect: "She howls when she hears music, just the most beautiful melody. But otherwise she could be an ambassador for dogs."

Shana, who grew to be 160 pounds, and the Fertigs became inseparable. They were together in an outer building on the property one warm October day when suddenly, the temperature dropped and snow began to fall. Within minutes, scores of trees cracked and fell, their limbs shattering from the sudden frost. The

> **CANINES** were the earliest animals to be domesticated, a process that began about 15,000 to 20,000 years ago.

OPPOSITE: *Shana saved the lives of Eve (right) and Norman (left) Fertig when the three were trapped in a sudden snowstorm.*

- Bear, a black Labrador retriever, saved his family's 14-month-old son, Stanley, from drowning after the toddler fell into the family pool. Bear jumped in the pool and held Stanley's head above the water until help arrived.
- Belle, a beagle, saved her owner's life by contacting 911 on his cell phone after he had a diabetic seizure and collapsed. Belle accepted the VITA Wireless Samaritan Award in 2006 for her courageous act and was the first canine to receive this honor.
- Toby, a golden retriever, saved his owner, Debbie, from choking to death on an apple. The dog jumped, pushing hard on her chest and forcing the apple out of her throat.

Fertigs stepped outside only to see that fallen trees had made it impossible for them to make their way back to their house. Then, a tree fell in front of the building they had just left, barring their way back in.

"I said to my husband, 'What do we do?' "

remembers Eve, who was 81 at the time. "And he said, 'We're trapped.' " The couple huddled together, trying to keep warm in the freezing temperatures. Then they noticed that Shana was busy burrowing. "She was digging a den as a wolf would dig a den, and then we lost sight of her," Eve recounts. "About half an hour later, we started hearing these howls and barks. She had made a tunnel back to the house, and wanted us to follow her, but we couldn't because it would only fit one person or a dog, and the branches from the trees were so dangerous."

When the couple didn't come as called, Shana crawled back through the trench she had built, returning to the couple with one leg pierced by branches. That injury still troubles her. "She was in bad shape," says Eve. "But she watched us argue about what we were going to do and then she just grabbed me by the sleeve and dragged me onto her back. I said, 'Norman—hang on to my ankle!' And she dragged us through the tunnel back home."

The fire chief, concerned about the octogenarians after neighbors couldn't reach

 on the card:

AMERICAN HEROES

Topps HERITAGE

AUTHENTIC USED BEDDING

SHANA   HERO DOG

Shana was honored with a Topps "American Heroes" trading card.

keep them warm. "We had no heat and no hot water, and they wanted to take us to the firehouse, but they said, 'Your wolf can't go.' And I said, 'If the wolf doesn't go, I don't go.' She had always shown us such incredible devotion. So they came back with food and a generator."

Only months later, Shana saved the day again when the Fertigs' furnace caught on fire; she dragged the sleeping couple out of bed and onto the porch. "She grabbed me by the nightgown and pulled me out to the porch, and then she went back for Norman. We called the fire chief and he said, 'What now?' " Eve remembers.

Norman passed away in 2011, as did their son, but Eve continues to have Shana's constant company. "She's always by my side. I don't have anyone to eat dinner with anymore, but Shana sits beside me, and she sleeps beside me every night. I have a bumper sticker on my car that says it all: 'Little Red Riding Hood Had It Wrong.' " ◆

them, arrived to find them collapsed on the porch, with Shana lying on top of them to

THE BIG BAD WOLF? There are many myths and misconceptions about wolves, partly thanks to fairy tales, such as "Little Red Riding Hood" and "The Three Little Pigs," that portray them as evil creatures. However, fairy-tale wolves are not representative of real wolves, which in the past hundred years have been responsible for only two human deaths in North America.

Rosie

GOLDEN RETRIEVER ◆ NEW YORK

The bond between a dog and a child is the stuff of legend, but the relationship between Rosie and Jessica made history in June 2011, when the 11-year-old golden retriever became the first courthouse dog in New York State. Sitting by Jessica's side on the witness stand, Rosie comforted, calmed, and encouraged the teenager as she testified against a family member accused of raping her over the course of years.

Consoling children wasn't the job Rosie was originally meant to do. Bred by Dale Picard and his wife, Lu, who together founded and run Educated Canines Assisting with Disabilities (ECAD), Rosie was meant to follow the path of her siblings and become a service dog. But within months, "it was clear that wasn't going to work," laughs Dale. "It took 90 days to teach her how to turn the light on, and then she wouldn't turn it off because her nose was so sensitive. When you would ask her to open the door, she'd look at you like, 'Oh, no—*you* open it and we will go through it together.' "

Rosie began to spend her days as Dale Picard's ambassador for ECAD at the Green Chimneys School in Brewster, New York, where the special-needs students train

IT'S BELIEVED that humans and dogs are so in tune that dogs can actually understand human emotions.

OPPOSITE: *Rosie, a golden retriever, helped witnesses recall traumatizing events through the program Courthouse Dogs.*

COURTROOM COMPANIONS

- Courthouse dogs are professionally trained assistance dogs who are graduates from service dog organizations. During criminal investigations and prosecutions, they help people suffering from physical, psychological, or emotional trauma.
- States with jurisdictions using courthouse dogs in the United States: Arizona, California, Colorado, Hawaii, Idaho, Indiana, Louisiana, Massachusetts, Missouri, New Mexico, New York, Ohio, Oklahoma, Pennsylvania, Tennessee, Texas, Utah, Virginia, Washington State.

the Picards' puppies to become service dogs. At Green Chimneys, Dale noticed Rosie's inherent talent for soothing children. "Rosie's great gift is she knows when a child is stressed . . . She can't stand for a kid to be sad, and will go to them to comfort them."

For the next eight years, while Picard worked with the children and the puppies, Rosie gravitated to the speech and occupational therapy rooms. The students were encouraged to talk by issuing Rosie one of the 80 verbal commands she knows. In physical therapy, the students would race after her over obstacles, rewarded by watching a dog do as they asked. "There are 'Tell' dogs, which is like a guide dog who tells you when to cross the street," explains Dale Picard. "Rosie would walk you right in front of a car. She's an 'Ask' dog; those are the dogs who will lie by your feet until you ask them to go get you your gloves. Then they'll get you those gloves and lie back down by your side."

These "Ask" qualities were precisely what Dr. David Crenshaw, the clinical director of the Children's Home of Poughkeepsie, in upstate New York, was looking for when he began supervising the case of Jessica, a then 15-year-old living at the facility. As the case against her accused rapist was being prepared to go to trial, Crenshaw began thinking about how to offer the traumatized teen comfort in court. He began reading about Courthouse Dogs, an organization founded by a former Washington State prosecutor, Ellen O'Neill-Stephens, and a veterinarian, Celeste Walsen, and dedicated to

Rosie and one of the many children she helped along the way

standardizing the use of facility dogs in the investigation and prosecution of crimes. "I want courthouse dogs to be as common as Dalmatians once were in firehouses," says O'Neill-Stephens, who first witnessed the calming effect that the trained dogs could have when she was working with juveniles.

"Trauma shuts down the verbal areas of the brain," explains Crenshaw, "and it's not only that you can't process what happened years later. It's that it's still hard to find the words to express what happened. Anxiety not only interferes with information processing but also with access to memory. The science of a dog in the courtroom is that the dog's presence reduces the stressed person's heart rate," he continues. "This reduces the automatic nervous system so kids don't freeze on the stand. Children with trauma history have such a high level of arousal that until you calm their

Rosie and her owner, Dale Picard, enjoy a walk on the beach.

systems, they simply can't process information." In addition, being near a dog stimulates the production of oxytocin, the "feel good" hormone released by nursing mothers.

Dale Picard, who received a call from Crenshaw after Courthouse Dogs passed his name along, knew that Rosie was the perfect dog for the job. "When a witness isn't stressed, the dog won't move," he says. "But the second the dog starts to feel the child's stress, it will look at the witness or wag its tail. If the child isn't answering the question, or the prosecutor comes back with a stronger tone, that will stress the child out, and the dog will rub her head or neck on the child's leg. If the pressure gets too strong, the dog will either take her nose and nudge the child's hand or come across her legs and try to put space between person and child."

For three months, Rosie and Jessica prepared by playing together, strengthening their bond for their day in the courtroom. Rosie had her work cut out for her, as she also had to learn to tolerate long stretches of sitting in the tight space of the witness stand. When her days with Jessica ended, she went home with her handler and sat in front of a chair, facing a barrier that moved closer every day until it simulated the witness box. "We were two days before the court date and we still didn't know if she could do it," remembers Picard.

The day of the trial, Jessica and Rosie arrived early and took their spot in the witness box so that Rosie wouldn't be seen by the jury and perhaps influence their feelings. "Jessica was petting Rosie the entire time," remembers Crenshaw, "and at one point during the hour she testified, Jessica took her shoe off and buried her foot in Rosie's fur, so the dog could [attempt to] read her heart rate. The prosecutor said, 'Is the man who raped you in the courtroom?' and we can assume Jessica's heart rate spiked, and she froze. She was just immobilized. Then Rosie put her head in Jessica's lap, and Jessica was able to lift her hand and point." The jury found the defendant guilty.

> " Rosie's great gift is she knows when a child is stressed. "

The legacy of the relationship between Jessica and Rosie is far greater than the verdict. Dr. Crenshaw has since adopted Rosie's younger sister, Ivy, as the in-house therapy dog at the Children's Home. "She has made the most extraordinary difference," says Crenshaw. "Troubled children will get down on the floor in a therapy session to lie with her, and the next thing you know they are recounting the horrors of their lives that they have never been able to share until now, thanks to the safety of being next to Ivy. And staff members who are stressed to the max will come and pet her for a few minutes and re-center. It's impossible to be with her and not feel calmer."

Rosie passed away in November 2012, but her effect on Jessica and many others lives on. ◆

A FURRY BEST FRIEND Dogs can be great companions for children. They can provide them unconditional love and friendship. An Australian study shows that children who grow up with dogs are more likely to maintain a healthy weight, and studies have linked owning pets with improved social skills and self-confidence.

Jasmine

GREYHOUND ◆ ENGLAND

No one ever expected Jasmine to love again. In 2003, English police officers discovered a greyhound cowering in a locked shed, severely malnourished and filthy, clearly abused. They drove her to the nearest place they could think of: the Nuneaton and Warwickshire Wildlife Sanctuary, founded and run by Geoff Grewcock with the intent of caring for sick and injured animals and birds. And so an act of fate would change the life of not only a dog and a person, but hundreds of other animals, as well.

"When I first met Jasmine, you could tell she had been emotionally devastated," Grewcock remembers. Determined to nurse her back to emotional and physical health, he and his staff showered her with affection. "Within a month, she became a loving dog," he says. "You could tell that she was a very gentle dog by nature. And then she started nurturing the other animals."

Her nurturing instinct first showed itself with Toby and Buster, a pair of abandoned puppies. When they arrived at the sanctuary, Jasmine approached as a mother dog would: licking

> **THE GREYHOUND** is one of the most ancient breeds, dating back to 2900 B.C.

OPPOSITE: *Jasmine, a rescued greyhound, cared for more than 50 animals including Bramble, an orphaned roe deer.*

- ORIGIN: **Egypt**
- COLOR(S): **Variety**
- HEIGHT: **27 to 30 inches**
- TEMPERAMENT: **Known for their incredible speed and sweet disposition. A great companion for families and other dogs, greyhounds show an independent streak, so patient training is required.**

them and picking them up in her mouth to carry them around the property. Then there was Roxy, a three-month-old fox found tied to a railing. "Jasmine seemed to know right away that the fox had been mistreated, and came up and started licking her," says Grewcock. "Roxy hated being left alone and would start to whine, and Jasmine would walk up to Roxy and lie beside her, and Roxy would stop immediately." Bramble, an orphaned 11-week-old fawn, received the same attention, as did five fox cubs, four badger cubs, fifteen chicks, eight guinea pigs, and fifteen rabbits.

"There are certain things only an animal mother can provide, and Jasmine provided it,"

says Grewcock. "She would nuzzle and lick the younger animals, which is especially important for young mammals such as foxes, badgers, and squirrels, who need a warm lick on their bellies to stimulate feeding and urinating."

Jasmine's love knew no boundaries: One of her favorites to cuddle with was Cleo, a Canada goose. And Parsley, another resident greyhound who wore a muzzle before Jasmine's arrival, became so attached to Jasmine that "all of his aggressiveness went away, and he never had to wear a muzzle again," recounts Grewcock. But always, at the end of Jasmine's day—and at the beginning—was Grewcock, who lives at the sanctuary. "She loved meeting new people, and would always come running out of the house to give them a friendly lick," he says. "I always knew I wanted to keep her, and I'm so glad I did."

Jasmine passed away in the fall of 2011, an event that was marked by a service where townspeople came to pay their respects. Then, "Emails and letters started flooding in from around the world, all out of respect

Jasmine and some of the animals in her care at the Nuneaton and Warwickshire Wildlife Sanctuary

to our wonderful greyhound," says Grewcock. The accompanying donations, upon which the sanctuary relies, have allowed Grewcock and his staff to continue the care they provide to the other mistreated animals at the sanctuary—if not with Jasmine's personal style, then at least in her name. "Her passing was so sad," says Grewcock, "but she was a legendary animal, and her legacy continues." ◆

KEEPING GOOD COMPANY The canine star Lassie, of the eponymous television series, was played by many similar-looking collies. Each Lassie had a canine companion or companions to keep them company on the set, including a pair of miniature poodles and a Jack Russell terrier.

Wendy

LABRADOODLE ◆ TEXAS

Elaine Heath never imagined owning a dog. Especially, she says, "a big black dog. I've never been a big dog lover." ◆ But she did love her retiree husband, Richard, very much, and years of chronic illnesses—including congestive heart failure and kidney and liver disease—were threatening the veteran's life. As for his *quality* of life, that had vanished long ago. Elaine embraced the idea of a service dog to provide constant companionship, and after Richard endured a particularly difficult three-week stay in the hospital, the couple came off the waiting list.

The dog selected for Richard was a black Labradoodle named Wendy. When the trainer brought her to the hospital for the family to meet her, "Wendy came into the room, walked right up to him, looked into his eyes, and put her head in his lap," Elaine says, still crying at the memory. "It was as if she was saying, 'Hi Dad, I'm home.' They were made for each other."

Immediately, Wendy's presence in the household changed Richard's daily routine. Instead of sitting in the same chair all day while his wife was at work, he was forced to move, even if just to feed Wendy and let her in and out to relieve

A SERVICE DOG'S training can begin as early as the second day of the puppy's life.

OPPOSITE: *Wendy, a Labradoodle, and Richard Heath share a special moment.*

- The goldendoodle is a cross between a golden retriever and a poodle. Breeders started to mix the two in the mid-1990s, and goldendoodles have become a fast favorite as family dogs.
- The Labradoodle comes from a mix of a Labrador retriever and a poodle. A retired veterinarian created the breed in the 1980s for an allergy sufferer who needed a service dog.
- The puggle is a mix of a pug and a beagle, bred in the 1980s as a companion dog. Puggles are known to have an exceptionally keen sense of smell.

a temporary catheter he needed to wear was about to overflow. "How in the world would she know *that?*" asks Elaine.

Still, nothing prepared the couple for Wendy's ingenuity the afternoon when Richard was working at the computer and suddenly found himself on the floor. As he later learned, he had suffered a stroke that left him partially paralyzed. "I remember Wendy trying to drag me into the living room, and somehow I got up into my chair there," he says. "That's when she brought me the telephone." Wendy is trained to fetch the phone, but only when asked, and what happened next was something her trainer says she never could have taught her: When Wendy saw that Richard couldn't dial with the hand she had placed the telephone in, she moved it to the other hand so he could call his wife.

Wendy's attention to Richard isn't just about duty, but about an inexplicable bond. Elaine rushed her husband to the hospital, "but I made a mistake and left Wendy at

herself. Wendy would pull him out of the chair with a tug rope to help him stand, and if he lost his balance, she would brace against him. She helped with the laundry, picking up whatever was dropped on the floor and placing it in the dryer, and, "unlike children, she puts her toys away," Elaine says with a laugh. Wendy also learned to alert to Richard's diabetes, letting him know if his levels were off; one evening, stationed at his bedside, she nudged him until he awakened to find that

Wendy and Heath enjoy a day at the Dallas Arboretum.

home. When I came back two hours later, she was in a panic, so I got her in the car and drove her to the hospital. I didn't direct or lead her, but she sniffed his scent through the ER and led us directly to his bed, where she lay down." All the more extraordinary: The room was empty, as Richard had been taken to another floor for tests. "If I hadn't seen it," says Elaine, "I wouldn't have believed it."

Elaine says that although her husband and Wendy are together around the clock, she never feels left out. "Richard is definitely her 'master,' but she is very devoted to me," she says. "She's just a part of us. This is now a marriage of three." ◆

SENSORY OVERLOAD Scientists think that a dog can distinguish smells 1,000 to 10,000 times better than a human. A dog gets most of its information from the scents it picks up. The area of the brain that identifies scents is 40 percent larger in dogs than it is in people.

Sonntag

GERMAN SHEPHERD ✦ WASHINGTON, D.C.

It was a scorching summer in Washington, D.C., when Ed Mulrenin, an attorney, decided that he and his dog Sonntag should get out of town. Far, far out of town. "We're going to Alaska!" Mulrenin remembers telling his canine best friend as he planned their six-week, 12,500-mile round-trip. ✦ But this adventure was more complicated than just throwing a couple of bags, a tent, and dog bowls in the car. The then 13-year-old German shepherd was paraplegic, suffering from a disc injury that had caused his paralysis two years earlier. Even though the dog had a custom-made cart that allowed him to be mobile, Mulrenin estimates that simply caring for Sonntag in the comfort of his home required at least three hours a day of dedicated care.

Despite the challenge, Mulrenin was fully committed. When he was offered his dream job, which would have meant moving to Russia without his dog, he turned it down. Euthanizing Sonntag was never an option—"I'm not putting a dog down just because he can't walk," says Mulrenin—but he recognized that both man and dog could use some fun. "I needed a goal to keep his

DOG CAMPING gear is widely varied. It includes safety vests, boots, and even backpacks that hold collapsible kennels.

OPPOSITE: *Sonntag and friend Richard Olsenius in Alaska*

55

GERMAN SHEPHERD

- ORIGIN: **Germany**
- COLOR(S): **Varies in color; strongly defined colors are preferable.**
- HEIGHT: **22 to 26 inches**
- TEMPERAMENT: **Fearless, intelligent, and eager to learn. Their loyalty, faithfulness, and courage make them good military or police dogs.**

"I remember driving into Denali National Park and all of a sudden Sonntag sparked up and pushed himself up on his front legs. It was like, 'Wow! The wilderness!' I remember that look on his face, like he was coming home. We were inseparable," he continues, "and I bonded with a dog in a way I had never thought imaginable."

Five months after the pair returned to Washington, the mobility of Sonntag's front legs began to falter, and Mulrenin called the veterinarian and made the difficult decision to put down his soul mate. Mulrenin says he has no regrets about the sacrifices he made for his beloved companion. "It was the first time in my life that I realized that I had actually been living under the principle *do what is right no matter what the consequences to me*. Those words are now permanently impressed on my mind and guide every important decision I make." ◆

spirit up. If you lose the dog's spirit, you lose the dog."

So the veteran campers headed off on an adventure into the wilderness: one at the wheel of the Land Rover, the other copiloting beside him in a custom-made bed. Although there were some hard times, including inclement weather and rocky terrain, Mulrenin says it was a trip of a lifetime.

ON THE ADVENTURE OF A LIFETIME Meriwether Lewis and William Clark had a canine companion on their Corps of Discovery expedition. Lewis most likely purchased his dog, Seaman, a Newfoundland breed, from a friend in Philadelphia for $20. Seaman proved useful in alerting the explorers to roaming buffalo or bears after dark.

Brock

DOBERMAN PINSCHER ♦ SOUTH CAROLINA

D ebi Boies, a founding member of the rescue group Doberman Assistance Network, had recently lost her 12-year-old Doberman and was looking to welcome another dog to her South Carolina horse farm. The dog had to have a gentle disposition and be able to get along with other animals, and when Boies heard about Brock, a young, scrawny Doberman, she knew he was the one. Used as a sparring partner for fighting dogs,

Brock had had his teeth filed down so that when he was attacked he couldn't fight back. Despite this mistreatment, the person fostering him "said he was kind, not aggressive with other animals, and only needed time to come out of his shell. I said, 'OK, we'll give it a try,'" remembers Boies. The only hitch: Brock was in Tampa, Florida.

Boies called friends to see if anyone would drive Brock to South Carolina. One friend, Jon Wehrenberg, responded with an even better offer: He'd pick Brock up with his private plane. "He said, 'Pilots love to fly, and we're always looking for an excuse,'" Boies remembers.

With Brock safely delivered to his new home, Wehrenberg asked Boies how she had spent years rescuing Dobermans without access to

PILOTS N PAWS made its largest rescue to date in 2012 by saving over 300 dogs from shelters where they may have been euthanized.

PAGE 59: *Brock, a Doberman pinscher, enjoys his new life with Debi Boies on her farm in South Carolina.*

DOBERMAN PINSCHER

- ORIGIN: **Unknown, possibly in Germany around 1900. The name came from a tax collector in Apolda, Louis Dobermann.**
- COLOR(S): **Black, red, blue, and fawn**
- HEIGHT: **24 to 28 inches**
- TEMPERAMENT: **Energetic, watchful, determined, alert, fearless, loyal, and obedient**

pilots. Boies acknowledged that ground transport is hard on dogs, and the logistics are exceedingly complicated. "Jon said, 'We need to do something.' I said, 'I know the rescue side, you know aviation,' and off we went. We had no idea what we were doing, but that was the beginning of Pilots N Paws."

Pilots N Paws now has an online community where rescuers communicate directly with the more than 3,000 participating pilots. The group has flown about 14,000 animals, including a Steppe eagle (a special request from a group of Navy SEALs), snakes, potbellied pigs, and even chickens between their rescue site and their forever homes. Nick O'Connell, a Pilots N Paws pilot and vice president of the board, says being able to unite the passion for flying with service is nothing less than addictive.

"The first flight I did were two chow puppies rescued from a dump. The adopters were at the airport, and everyone was so happy and crying, and I thought, 'I can't wait to do this again.'" The personal cost—about $100 an hour for fuel for his plane—"ain't cheap," he admits. "But you'll scrape together the money to do it."

Now a nonprofit so pilots can deduct some expenses, Pilots N Paws is an accomplishment for which Boies constantly thanks Brock, who has become a profusely affectionate companion. "I'm so grateful to him," she says. "The hell he went through, and the place he came from, but here is a dog who has unknowingly saved thousands upon thousands of lives." ◆

SAVING THE LIVES OF OUR FURRY COMPANIONS According to the Humane Society of the United States, 30 years ago the euthanasia rate of dogs and cats in relation to the number of dogs and cats kept as pets was around 25 percent. Today, the euthanasia rate has dramatically decreased to about 3 percent.

Chancer

GOLDEN RETRIEVER ◆ GEORGIA

The joy a dog found in comforting a boy has transformed the Winokur family, whose adopted son, Iyal, displays symptoms of fetal alcohol syndrome (FAS). With damage to his brain impacting his behavior, the teenager's rages, delayed emotional growth, and sleepless nights were undoing a family exhausted by nearly a decade of round-the-clock care. Desperate, Iyal's mother, Donnie Winokur, began investigating dogs trained to work with autistic children, who can present challenges like those of children with FAS, and decided to take a leap of faith. Soon, the family became the owners of the first certified assistance dog trained for someone living with FAS.

Within two weeks after Iyal was paired with Chancer, a golden retriever, the family's lives were transformed. On their first night together, Chancer saw Iyal in a hotel hot tub and took a racing leap into the water, determined to save the boy he thought was drowning. "Somehow he knew that Iyal was his boy, and he had rescued him," says Winokur. "I don't know how he knew, but he did." On Chancer's first night in the Winokurs' home, he crawled into Iyal's bed to

GOLDEN RETRIEVERS are popular service dogs because of their friendly nature, midsize height, and inclination to fetch dropped items.

OPPOSITE: *Chancer, a golden retriever, and Iyal have a special bond.*

STUPENDOUS SENSES

- Dogs *can* see color, but their sense of color is much duller than ours.
- Our furry friends can hear sounds almost twice as well as humans and use fifteen different muscles to move their ears.

sleep beside him; for the first time, after years of nocturnal disruption, the entire family slept until the sun came up.

Selected in part for his great self-confidence, Chancer isn't put off by Iyal's rages. Instead, when the anger begins to build, he burrows close, butting open Iyal's tightening arms until he can nestle in and soothe him. "The rages don't escalate the way they used to, and they don't last as long," says Winokur. "Sometimes when he [Iyal] gets upset, he hand-claps—but now he can do it into Chancer's fur, and that will calm Iyal in a sensory way. Somehow, Chancer has learned it's one of his jobs."

Chancer has also learned to sense when Iyal's temper escalates even if he's as much as two floors away from Iyal. "Somehow he will pick up on it and go to Iyal wherever he is and just hang there with him," says Winokur. This isn't surprising to Julie Hecht of the Horowitz Dog Cognition Lab at Barnard College.

Hecht points to dogs' extraordinary auditory abilities, explaining that Chancer would be able to hear Iyal begin to mutter—how his rages often present themselves—even at a great distance. What Hecht finds unusual is Chancer's motivation to comfort Iyal and his enthusiasm in doing so. "This is a dog who is very attentive and enjoys doing his job," she says. "And most important, he really enjoys his relationship with Iyal."

Chancer also makes it easier for the family to enjoy their relationships with the teenager. "I have a child with a severe disability but a huge, kind heart and soul—and it's about making sure we have access to that heart and soul," says Winokur. And there are newfound moments of peace. "Now, if Iyal drops to the floor and starts writhing I can say, 'Go find Chancer,' and he will put his head on him and Chancer absorbs a lot of that energy. Before Chancer, it was impossible to have two minutes of nothingness. Now we can."

Chancer is beloved by all members of the

Chancer is the first service–trained dog for people living with FAS.

family—Winokur and Morasha, Iyal's sister, have written children's books about him—and Winokur credits him with helping her spiritually and emotionally. "We were just so raw after all these years, because it requires so much understanding of the invisible chaos that goes on with Iyal," she says. "But he enlightens me about interspecies connections." Still, Chancer does have his flaws. "He gets overexcited and will hump the furniture," says Winokur with a laugh. "And he's a counter cruiser who will eat absolutely anything you leave out. No matter how extraordinary he is, you can't take the dog out of the service dog." ◆

THE BENEFITS OF A SERVICE DOG Service dogs can provide great support to children born with FAS. Service dogs have been shown to improve self-confidence and independence as well as both abstract and concrete thinking. They can also help to sharpen the child's focus and increase his or her attention span.

Willow

MIXED BREED ◆ NEW YORK

O nce your dog has conquered horseback riding and skateboarding, and learned upwards of 250 visual and verbal commands, why not teach her how to read? "It was either that or learning how to make a martini," jokes Lyssa Howells, who was looking to teach her gifted dog, a little brown, black, and white terrier mix named Willow, some new tricks. ◆ Spurred on by a bet with a friend, Howells wrote three commands on separate pieces of paper—"Sit Up," "Wave," and "Bang" (in response, Willow rolls over on her back as if she's been shot)— and used food rewards to teach Willow to do what each written cue asked of her, in a matter of six weeks. "It's repetition, just like anything," says Howells, who is a dog trainer. "She learned to understand that particular order of letters, whether they were hand-written or typed. What she's recognizing is the meaning of a pattern of pictures, which is really what reading is."

Howells also trained Willow to recognize the quantities of "more" or "less": When asked to point to the hand in which Howells holds a larger or smaller quantity of something, she is unerring whether

A BONOBO called Panbanisha had a vocabulary of 3,000 words. She typed these words onto a computer that produced a synthetic voice.

OPPOSITE: *Willow, a mixed breed, not only knows 250 verbal and visual commands, she also knows how to read.*

- The first dog ever to walk the tightrope was an American Eskimo named Stout's Pal Pierre, in the Barnum and Bailey Circus.
- Jesse, a Jack Russell terrier, is a YouTube star who demonstrates helpful tricks like pushing a shopping cart, putting away his toys, answering the telephone, and even working out!
- Uggie, a Jack Russell terrier, performed tricks like "speaking," walking on two legs, bowing, playing dead, and acting bashful in the hit movies *The Artist* and *Water for Elephants*.

Howells holds peas, carrots, or cookies. Howells has trained other dogs to do the same by teaching them to recognize the difference between an empty hand and a hand full of treats. "She's just really brilliant," says Howells. "She will put her paw on her food bowl when she is hungry. I can ask her to go into certain rooms and get me specific items, like,

'Can you please go to the kitchen and grab me a pen?' and she will."

Howells takes her best friend with her everywhere, including to training sessions with other dogs, where she uses Willow as an intentional distraction for the dogs she's teaching to sit and stay. "I'll be teaching a dog a command and Willow will be doing it at the same time," says Howells. "The hardest thing I've ever had to teach her is how *not* to listen to me." ◆

Willow can read basic commands like "sit" and "wave."

HOW MUCH LANGUAGE CAN DOGS UNDERSTAND? Dogs understand humans better than we may think, even though they are unrelated to us. During the domestication process, the dog's brain adapted to become more attuned to humans and their signals.

Henry

LABRADOR RETRIEVER ◆ TENNESSEE

Henry has spent a decade expressing his adoration for his master, Frank Walker. The chocolate Lab always sits beside Walker in his truck or in the golf cart he uses to get around his Tennessee property; he sleeps at the foot of the bed, and he even taught himself how to alert Walker to the seizures from which he occasionally suffers. Several minutes before a seizure happens, "he'll nudge me or bark to get my attention to make sure I know and can get to a safe place," says Walker. But Henry's stalwart devotion shone through the day he saved Walker's life.

On a warm February day, Walker decided to cut down a dead tree behind his house. This was yard work he had often done before on his property. This time, however, the tree fell toward him, and Walker was pinned to the ground. "I had my cell phone, but my coat was five feet away with the phone in it," he remembers. "I couldn't move, and I knew I had cracked ribs. My arm and legs were twisted like a pretzel."

For three hours Walker lay there, bleeding from internal injuries and growing weaker

LABRADOR RETRIEVERS are the most popular service dogs, thanks to their generally friendly nature and gentle demeanor.

NEXT PAGE: *Henry and his owner, Frank Walker*

LABRADOR RETRIEVER

- LIFE EXPECTANCY: **About 10 to 12 years**
- BREED HISTORY: **Native to Newfoundland, Labradors were crossed with other hunting dogs over time to improve their hunting skills.**
- CHARACTERISTICS: **Labs seem to enjoy having a job to do and want to feel like a member of the family. Many Labradors excel as guide and search-and-rescue dogs.**
- FIRST JOB: **Helping fishermen pull in nets from icy water**

saving run for it. "I had a new neighbor who I had met the month before," says Walker. "I introduced him to the dog in my truck and said, 'If you see him without me, you'll know something is wrong.'" When the neighbor came into sight, Henry began barking wildly; when the neighbor didn't respond, Henry raced for the man, bringing him back to Walker's side.

Walker was flown to the Vanderbilt University Medical Center, where he was found to have seven cracked ribs, a ruptured spleen, three fractures to his femur, a broken upper arm, and a smashed hand. Treatment involved ten hours of surgery and a medically induced coma. When Walker finally returned home, he and his wife made sure to thank Henry for his heroism. "We got him a lot of treats," he says, "And we give him a *lot* of love. He's my godsend." ◆

by the minute. Henry stayed by his side, helping keep him alert and warm. "I was doing a lot of praying and thinking about ways I was going to survive," says Walker. Then, his dog—who had been trained never to leave the property on his own—made a life-

HOW DID HENRY KNOW SOMETHING WAS WRONG? A dog's sense of smell is a thousand times better than a human's, so it's no wonder that a dog can warn its owner of an epileptic seizure, low blood sugar, a heart attack, and even some types of cancer. Scientists do not know whether any given dog breed is better than another at sniffing out medical problems.

Luca

PIT BULL ◆ NEW YORK

Sometimes, in order to really listen, it helps when you can't hear anything at all. That's the case with Luca, a deaf pit bull whose gift as a therapy dog stems from what others might perceive as a disability. ◆ Luca, who was adopted as a puppy from a shelter, was trained early on by his owners, Brooke Slater-Goldstein and Dave Goldstein, to make constant eye contact so he could follow their signed commands. For the at-risk or disabled youths with whom Luca now interacts as a therapy dog, that can often mean feeling—and being—recognized for the first time. "He doesn't give these kids a choice but to make eye contact, because he walks right up to them and demands it," says Slater-Goldstein. "There was one student who had emotional issues and was rocking back and forth. Luca walked right up to him to see what he was doing and the kid looked up, and smiled, and stopped.

Another person who had never taken a step without his walker moved away from it for the first time on his own to pet Luca, who was staring at him from across the room and wagging his tail. Humans can't do this. Humans have tried and haven't come close."

Interestingly, despite their close genetic relations to

DOGS MAY be born deaf because of genetic defects, may become deaf due to injury or infection, or may experience hearing loss as they age.

OPPOSITE: *Even though Luca is deaf he has learned to follow his owners' instructions by their special hand signals.*

- In 1903, two men and a dog completed the first cross-country American road trip: Horatio Jackson, Sewall Crocker, and Jackson's pit bull, Bud. Bud wore specially made driving goggles and helped keep an eye out for bumps in the road.
- Because they were so popular in early 20th-century America, pit bulls were used by many companies for advertising. One of the most famous is the RCA dog, a fox terrier–bull terrier mix.
- Many famous Americans have owned pit bulls, including President Theodore Roosevelt, President Woodrow Wilson, Helen Keller, Mark Twain, Thomas Edison, and Fred Astaire.

domesticated dogs, neither can wolves: A study published in *Current Biology* in 2003 found that socialized wolves, unlike dogs, generally avoid looking at humans' faces. This led the researchers to posit that "the readiness of dogs to look at the human face has led to complex forms of dog-human communication."

Luca follows commands by watching Slater-Goldstein and Goldstein and their hand signals, which make up a unique sign language—some of which is similar to American Sign Language and some of which is invented ("Good boy," for example, is a wriggled thumb). Slater-Goldstein and Goldstein tell Luca whom to make eye contact with by pointing at the person he should look at or approach. "He knows eight to ten commands," says Slater-Goldstein. "We cut out all the excess that people don't even realize is just extra verbiage when it comes to training a dog. And we communicate with him via body language. I smile and his tail wags; I give him, 'Mommy face' and he knows he's been bad and lies right down."

Luca inspired Slater-Goldstein and Goldstein to start Bruised Not Broken, a nonprofit organization and advocacy group devoted to pit bull rescue that has more than 200,000 fans on Facebook. The three are now planning to tour college campuses to help change people's minds about the breed. They are also continuing to work with adolescents. "We are part of a program that teaches empathy and compassion. When Luca walks in the room and they see a pit bull, these 15-year-olds hit the

Luca inspired the organization Bruised Not Broken to help correct misconceptions about pit bulls.

deck screaming," Slater-Goldstein says with a laugh. "So the first lesson is, 'No prejudice. Decide how you feel after spending time with him.' And then they start learning hand signals, and he's following their commands, and they are really connecting with him. He takes them seriously. And they, in turn, take him seriously."

Slater-Goldstein says that Luca is tired at the end of a day of therapy, but there is some recompense: Thanks to his deafness, he falls into a deep sleep utterly undisturbed by the noises of city life. "The work he does," says Slater-Goldstein, "this is what he was born to do." ◆

READING HUMAN EMOTIONS A UK study shows that dogs, like humans, exhibit a "left gaze bias" when looking at a human face. The right side of the human face tends to be better at expressing emotion, so when looking at a face the eye tends to drift left. Dogs may have developed this left gaze bias so that they could better read human emotions.

Faith

MIXED BREED ◆ INDIANA

Jude Stringfellow was used to her children bringing home animals in need, but the puppy her son carried into the house in 2003 really upped the ante. The three-week-old female part-chow puppy he had rescued from a nearby flea market required around-the-clock care and attention. Then there was the matter of her legs: She had been born with three, only two of which worked. (And her single front leg had to be amputated when she was seven months old.)

"Shortly before my son brought Faith home, we had found baby ducks and tried to nurse them, but it hadn't worked out," remembers Stringfellow. "So I prepared my three kids and said, 'The dog may not make it through the night.' My daughter said, 'Can we make sure the time she has is as good as possible?' and I said we could."

That turned out to be under-optimistic: At six weeks old, Faith was sitting up on her haunches. When she was three months old, annoyed by another dog in the house teasing her by nipping at her,

> **FAITH APPEARED** on *The Oprah Winfrey Show* twice, in 2006 and 2010, and was called Oprah's "all-time favorite" animal guest.

OPPOSITE: *Faith, despite being born with deformed front legs, has learned to walk upright.*

Laura Stringfellow plays with Faith (far right) and their other family dog.

Faith stood tall on her back legs and took off after him, running as a person would. "She was like a kangaroo, leaping over chairs and sometimes clearing them and sometimes not," Stringfellow remembers. "She had to learn her boundaries, and how strong her back legs were."

With Faith off and running, Stringfellow began taking her to nursing homes and hospitals. When a family member of a patient in a hospital suggested that disabled members of the military might love to meet Faith, Stringfellow began taking her to local veterans hospitals. They then traveled to Wash-

- A fall out of a third-story window shattered the front legs of a six-month-old pit bull named London. The legs had to be amputated, and it was determined he would be fitted with a front wheelchair. While waiting for his wheelchair, London has learned to walk on his two back legs.
- Chihuahua siblings Moose and Maverick were born without their front legs and abandoned at a young age. Adopted by a veterinarian, the brothers work on two legs as therapy dogs at shelters and assisted living centers, showing that it is all right to be different.

ington, D.C., and Virginia, and to bases around the world. Faith, who has been made an honorary sergeant in the U.S. Army for her work, has provided joy as well as healing to those she visited. "When she's there, the veterans will talk about what happened to them," Stringfellow says. "And sometimes, they can't put it into words and just sit there and cry. Faith knows how to help; sometimes she just sits and listens, and sometimes she crawls into their laps."

Faith isn't the only member of the family who has found her calling: Stringfellow has given motivational speeches about the many lessons that Faith has to teach, and has also written the book *Faith Walks*, with a percentage of the proceeds going to charity. "Faith is what it looks like to be positive and persevere, and no matter how many times someone comes up to pet her, she acts like she's never been petted before." Her generosity has been contagious, especially for those closest to her. "I wasn't necessarily compassionate before I got her, and I didn't necessarily go out of my way to help people," says Stringfellow. "Now I do." ◆

HOW IS IT POSSIBLE FOR A DOG TO WALK ON TWO LEGS? Dogs that are born with only two legs quickly adapt to their disability. Dogs who unfortunately lose their legs later in life can still learn to compensate for their lost limbs. The inner ear helps them balance and the muscles in the other legs gain additional strength as they help the dog move.

Effie

MIXED BREED ◆ MICHIGAN

S ave a life and have yours saved in return. It's not often that the universe offers up such literal recompense, but it did in the case of three women whose rescue dogs detected their cancer. ◆ Effie, a large, stray brown-and-white mixed breed, didn't seem especially promising. "She had every parasite known to dogdom, she dug holes in the yard, she cowered when men came around, and she growled at children," says Lisa Hulber, who lives in Port Huron, Michigan. "She was really unadoptable." But Hulber fell in love with her anyway and rescued her. The favor was soon returned. Four months after Hulber had a routine mammogram with normal results, Effie began persistently sticking her nose into Hulber's breast. "I would push her away and she'd keep doing it," Hulber remembers, "and I knew it wasn't right." Concerned, Hulber went back for another mammogram; again, it came back normal. Still convinced something was not right, she went for an ultrasound, and her family doctor found an aggressively growing, large carcinoma of a type that rarely shows up on mammograms.

Hulber scheduled a double mastectomy for a

DOGS ARE ABLE to pick up chemicals in concentrations of a few parts per trillion; this may enable them to smell tumors on humans' breath.

OPPOSITE: *Effie successfully sniffed out the breast cancer of her owner, Lisa Hulber.*

79

A LIFE-SAVING SENSE OF SMELL

- The medical journal *The Lancet* was the first to report a cancer-sniffing dog. In 1989 the journal recounted the story of a woman whose border collie–Doberman mix persistently sniffed at a mole that was later diagnosed as a malignant melanoma.
- In 2002, Tangle, a brown cocker spaniel, became one of the first dogs in the world to take part in cancer-sniffing research.
- Dogs' noses have as many as 300 million olfactory receptors; humans possess about 6 million. In addition, their noses separate smelling and breathing. Our noses only allow us to breathe and smell in the same inhalation.

month later, during which time Effie began sniffing under her arm. Hulber showed the doctor the precise spot Effie had fixated on, and when she awoke from surgery she was informed that Effie had been right. "Of 27 lymph nodes, that was the only node it had spread to," she says. "The nurse, head surgeon, and I were all bawling our eyes out about this stupid dog. A lot of women cry about losing their breasts, but what makes me cry is the gift this dog gave me."

Dogs' ability to sniff out cancer is being studied by researchers who are training them to identify specific forms of the disease. Dr. Michael McCulloch is research director of the Pine Street Foundation, a northern California clinic that published a study asserting that it had trained five dogs to detect lung cancer in people's breath with 99 percent accuracy. When it came to breast cancer, with respect to which the researchers had a smaller number of samples, the dogs were right approximately 88 percent of the time with no false positives. McCulloch is now studying dogs' ability to sniff out ovarian cancer. "Dogs' sense of smell is quite acute, and when tumors develop in the body, odors emanating may be exuded locally or regionally via diffusion across the skin or in perspiration," he explains.

As for the untrained dogs' ability to alert their owners to cancer, McCulloch points to the need of pack animals to assess each other's health through scent in order to survive. "There is a modern example with wolves and sled dogs," he says. "The dogs have to be fit in order to run with the pack, so they are probably using the same skills with their human companions. When they smell other dogs, they are asking, 'How healthy are you?'"

In a similar story, Carol Witcher's boxer rescue, Floyd Henry, alerted her by nipping at her nose and then pawing her right breast. "I thought, 'Oh boy, we've got a problem,'" remembers Witcher, who lives outside Atlanta, Georgia. She was found to have breast cancer, for which she had a lumpectomy. And Linda Botwinick's rescued beagle-Lab mix began nosing and pawing her owner's left breast less than six months after a routine mammogram. "Like most women, I thought I had a free pass for a year," says Botwinick, who lives in Boca Raton, Florida. She immediately returned to the doctor, who found a tumor so aggressive it had developed into a menacing mass in less than two months. Botwinick had a lumpectomy, followed by chemotherapy

Floyd Henry and Carol Witcher share a hug.

and radiation. "I'm so grateful to my dog, and to the fact that I listened to her," she says. "She really is my angel. I saved her life, and then she saved mine." ◆

TEACHING OLD DOGS NEW TRICKS A 2006 study by the Pine Street Foundation indicated that dogs could sniff out breast cancers with 88 percent accuracy even in the earliest stages of the disease. A 2011 study described a Belgian shepherd dog who was able to detect prostate cancer in human urine with a 91 percent success rate.

Pearl

LABRADOR RETRIEVER ◆ CALIFORNIA

Shortly after Pearl was surrendered to a California shelter by her owner, the black Lab was rescued by an organization that trains service dogs for the blind. "Halfway through testing her, the rescue said, 'This dog is way too hyper to be a Seeing Eye dog,' " recounts Pearl's handler, Los Angeles firefighter Captain Ron Horetski. ◆ That was music to the ears of the National Disaster Search Dog Foundation, which needs dogs for search-and-rescue missions requiring around-the-clock work and a "Wait—I'm just getting going!" attitude. Founded in 1996, the Ojai, California–based organization trains and then pairs dogs with firefighters and other first responders to aid in disasters like the 9/11 attacks. Thirteen SDF-trained dogs were deployed to work in the rubble of the World Trade Center.

Before being assigned to Horetski, Pearl underwent a battery of tests and training.

All dogs have a sense of smell tens of thousands of times more sensitive than humans', but search dogs need more than just a sense of smell. For Pearl, there were x-rays to make sure that her hips and shoulders could withstand walking on rubble; tests to make sure she was willing to traverse shaky

161 SEARCH- and-rescue dogs from all over the world assisted in the aftermath of the 2010 earthquake in Haiti.

OPPOSITE: *Pearl, a Labrador retriever, is a search-and-rescue dog who helps after natural and man-made disasters.*

LABRADOR RETRIEVER

- **GENERAL APPEARANCE:** Strongly built, athletic, well-balanced, medium-sized dog
- **COAT:** Short, straight, and very dense
- **AVERAGE SIZE:** 55 to 75 pounds
- **POPULARITY:** The Labrador retriever is one of the most popular breeds in the United States.

surfaces, which dogs generally avoid; and encounters to ensure she was at ease with unfamiliar people and dogs. "Search dogs are completely different than working dogs like the ones who sniff for drugs in the airport, or bomb-sniffing dogs who are by their handlers' sides at all times," says Janet Reineck, Ph.D., an executive at the organization. "Search dogs are off the leash, and they need to be directed from a long way away, and also to be able make their own decisions. It's an incredibly complex set of skills."

After seven months of training, Pearl was assigned to Horetski, and the two began an arduous year of training together. The FEMA certification test requires the dog to search a 6,000- and a 15,000-square-foot rubble pile with four to six "victims" hidden in the two piles; other items such as food and clothing are also hidden as distractions. The dogs have 20 minutes to search each pile, and the dog can't miss more than one of the "victims"; if the dog alerts to any object other than the human, the dog fails. Thanks to her go-go attitude and intense focus, Pearl aced the test.

But there was little time to celebrate: On January 12, 2010, 17 days after Pearl's graduation, an enormous earthquake hit Haiti, and Pearl and Horetski were deployed as part of a canine search-and-rescue team. "It was like a war zone. Everywhere there were crushed buildings. I remember looking around and thinking, 'Where do we even start?'" says Horetski. "You find someone buried five floors below, and it takes 12 to 38 hours to get them out. Pearl had to climb over dead bodies and human remains. And because it was so hot, I had to give her IVs of fluid just to keep her hydrated."

Hard at work in Haiti, Pearl looks for survivors of the earthquake in the rubble.

Pearl and Horetski, along with other teammates, recovered 12 survivors during their mission. Dogs can detect the presence of a body where people can't, thanks to their stunning olfactory skills; James Walker, the former director of the Sensory Research Institute at Florida State University, found that dogs' sense of smell is thousands of times more powerful than that of humans, allowing rescue dogs like Pearl to go where no man can (at least in a sensory way). At first, Haitians, who are generally unaccustomed to dogs as pets, had been terrified by Pearl and her canine colleagues. But by the end of the team's stay in Haiti, says Horetski, "they were walking up and giving us hugs. Watching

Pearl with her handler, Captain Ron Horetski

Pearl do what she was trained to do—it was just awesome."

Pearl had a chance to shine again when the devastating tsunami hit Japan in March 2011. Working in snow and rain, and in temperatures that never rose above the 50s, was physically and emotionally grueling. "We came across a lot of people, but we didn't find any life," Horetski says quietly. But Pearl never displayed signs of depression. "This is a working dog, doing her work," he explains.

At home, the pair's lives are simpler. Horetski plans to eventually retire from the fire department, but for now there are still biweekly training sessions in rubble and in abandoned buildings, local search-and-rescue missions, and long days at the firehouse. Pearl accompanies her handler 24/7, as part of the program's guidelines, and has no shortage of affection for her many fans—although Horetski is not one of those fawning over her. "She's a work dog, so she's not on my lap watching TV at night," he says. "And we don't go to the dog run to play, because she needs to be ready and have the energy for an emergency. But she's so much more . . . She's my partner." ◆

A HISTORY OF HELPING St. Bernards were the first dogs used for search-and-rescue work. The monks at Great St. Bernard Hospice, situated in the Alps between Italy and Switzerland, acquired St. Bernards sometime between 1660 and 1670. The dogs searched for snow-buried travelers and provided warmth to injured people.

Chaser

Most dog owners suspect their pets are geniuses. But some dogs, it must be admitted, have a tad more genius than the rest. Consider Chaser, a border collie who belongs to Professor Emeritus John W. Pilley, of Wofford College. Thanks to intensive training by Pilley, who has a Ph.D. in animal learning, Chaser has learned to comprehend more than a thousand proper nouns. When asked, not only will she pick a specific object out from many, she will perform the requested action with the object, such as pawing it, licking it, or taking it.

As a professor, Pilley spent years trying to teach dogs language, and had failed. "I remember before I got her, I was sitting around a campfire with farmers who had border collies and I said, 'Your dogs don't *really* know their names. When you use their name, all they know is to look at you and come to you.' The farmers looked at me like the idiot Ph.D. professor that I was. The fact is, I just hadn't been successful in teaching the [dogs] yet."

When Pilley read a study about a border collie in Germany who had

BORDER COLLIES, with extraordinary instincts and unrivaled abilities to reason, can work out of sight of their handlers, without specific commands.

PAGE 89: *Chaser, a border collie, has learned more than 1,000 words, including the names of her toys.*

BORDER COLLIE

- ORIGIN: **Border between Scotland and England**
- COLOR(S): **Typically black and white**
- HEIGHT: **18 to 22 inches**
- TEMPERAMENT: **The border collie is a highly energetic dog, needing extensive exercise daily. Border collies are fiercely loyal family dogs and may be reserved with strangers.**

learned to recognize more than 300 items by name, he was determined to try again with his own border collie. The breed is known for intelligence and the drive to work. This time, he decided, he would raise the puppy using a technique that involved continually repeating the name of an object. Chaser began training up to five hours a day when she was only eight weeks old, and by the time she was six months old, says Pilley, "she was learning names of objects so rapidly we suspected

she was learning a name in one five-minute trial." Within three years, her ability to associate a name with an object included 800 cloth animals, 116 balls, 26 Frisbees, and a plethora of plastic items.

"One of my trainers said, 'If you give your heart to a dog, the dog will give her mind to you,'" says Pilley. "Dogs are smarter than we think they are, and dogs have a greater possibility for learning language than we realize. But it takes a good teacher to teach a dog, and we are still working on developing methods that enable us to teach them language."

Pilley and Chaser have scaled back but still hold morning training sessions on the campus of the Spartanburg, South Carolina, college where Pilley taught for 30 years. Border collies, bred to herd sheep, have tremendous energy, and, says Pilley, "they will drive their owners crazy if they don't have work to do. Training is all play for her. Everything is play for her. Sometimes," he admits, "I go to sleep at 8 p.m., just to get a rest from her." ◆

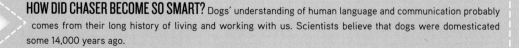

HOW DID CHASER BECOME SO SMART? Dogs' understanding of human language and communication probably comes from their long history of living and working with us. Scientists believe that dogs were domesticated some 14,000 years ago.

Dutchess

MIXED BREED ◆ OREGON

Rachael Scdoris doesn't have one favorite dog; she has a hundred. That's how many dogs it takes for this sled dog racer (or musher) from Bend, Oregon, to train for the Iditarod—the annual 1,049-mile race from Anchorage to Nome, Alaska, which she first entered in 2005. All mushers rely on their dogs for guidance, but Scdoris is more reliant than most. Born with a rare vision disorder that makes her nearsighted, farsighted, and color-blind, Scdoris was eight when she first articulated her dream of racing the Iditarod. "It was quite simple, really," she remembers. The daughter of a sled dog trainer, "I grew up with sled dogs, and my parents always told me the sky's the limit. But they did ask me how I was going to navigate the trail. I said, 'We'll have headsets.' "

Scdoris was racing dogs by the time she was 11, and in 2006, with a time of 12 days, 10 hours, and 42 minutes spent on the trail, she became the first blind athlete to finish the Iditarod. Throughout it, and all the races that followed, her dogs have been her inspiration.

"There's something that is quite common in distance racing, when you are racing at night and start to think, 'You should be sleeping now in

> **SLED DOGS** are bred for their strength, speed, feet, attitude, desire to pull, and ability to run within a team.

OPPOSITE: *Despite being legally blind, Rachael Scdoris competes in the 2005 Iditarod with the help of her sled dog team.*

Scdoris and her "soul dog," Dutchess, who helped guide her on the trail

a warm bed,' but I can just look down at my team and see their tails wagging. I can't help but be happy with them when I see how happy they are to be running." And when Scdoris is in training and feels like taking a day off, "I do it for them," she says. "I think, 'I'll give them a little something today.' "

Although her dogs aren't pets, Scdoris is unreserved in her love for them. During a race, she massages them at every stop; in addition to being kind, this helps her get a sense of how their muscles are holding up, since she can't visually assess their physical condition. She has even been known to sing to them. "I take the best dogs on races," she says. "There is a special bond with every dog, who all have their individual quirks. There's one, Yoda, who most of the time doesn't like me unless there is

- The Iditarod is a 1,049-mile-long race along the historic Iditarod Trail, starting in Anchorage and ending in Nome, Alaska.
- Today, mushers participate with teams of 12 to 16 dogs. It takes racers 10 to 17 days to complete.
  - The Iditarod Trail had its beginnings as a mail and supply route, originally traveled by dogsled.

a potential to go for a ride in the dog truck or run. But they all trust me enough to hit the wall and keep running if I ask them. I never push them to a point where they are tired. In training, I never run them more than seven hours."

Most of Scdoris's dogs are what she calls "Alaskan Huskies," which, she explains, are "technically northern mutts who love to run. It's not a registered breed." What does

Scdoris look for in her dogs? "A combination of heart and athletic ability."

The dog who perhaps best embodied these traits was Dutchess, whom Scdoris still calls "my great leader" even though she passed away in 2008. Dutchess accompanied Scdoris when she was a teenager on the 500-mile Wyoming Stage Stop, a race she describes as so long, "I was 15 when I started it and it ended when I was 16."

"Dutchess had a mind of her own," she says. "She'd look at me like, 'I know you think this is where we should go.' She wasn't usually right," she says with affection. "She got me into a lot of trouble, but she also got me out of a lot of trouble." Dutchess died too young to enjoy what Scdoris's other dogs do in retirement: moving into her house full-time with free rein over the couch and the opportunity to play ball in the warm confines of the living room. Still, she did share her owner's bed when they traveled together. "Dutchess," says Scdoris, "dazzled everybody." ◆

STAYING WARM IN THE ALASKA WILDERNESS Different breeds of dogs have different coats. Sled dogs have good fur with an undercoat and an overcoat. The undercoat serves to insulate the dogs from cold temperatures, and the overcoat discourages ice and snow from building up on their fur during windy and cold conditions.

Izzy

Gabrielle Ford calls Izzy her "second life." That's because in her adolescence, before the coonhound came into her life, Ford was so afraid of being bullied that she loathed being in public. ◆ Ford was diagnosed at the age of 12 with a rare muscle disease, Friedreich's ataxia; by the time she graduated from high school, her condition had advanced so much that she fell while crossing the stage to accept her diploma. When her fellow students made fun of her for the tumble, Ford confined herself to her family's house and refused to leave. Then, at the age of 20, by now relying on a wheelchair, she asked her parents if she could have a dog to help assuage her loneliness.

"I said she could, but that she would be accountable in every way," remembers Ford's mother, Rhonda Kay Hillman. "I knew that even if it was just letting the dog in and out the back door, the movement would keep her muscles going."

The excitement of getting Izzy, says Ford, was enough to shake her out of her long depression. "The month before she arrived, I went out to buy her all this stuff and I could feel myself

WHERE THE RED FERN GROWS is a famous children's book that features coonhounds. The book shows the loyalty, intelligence, and friendliness of the breed.

OPPOSITE: *Izzy gave her owner, Gabrielle Ford, the courage to speak out about her experience of being bullied.*

Izzy and Gabrielle were best friends and constant companions.

coming out of my shell," she remembers. "And when Izzy came home, it was like night and day. I wasn't just taking care of her, I was now taking care of myself. I felt so comfortable with her. I could talk to her about anything, and she was my best friend and my confidante."

When Izzy was less than a year old, she was diagnosed with a liver condition that necessitated surgery. Two years later, she was also diagnosed with a rare muscular disease the symptoms of which mirrored her owner's, including fatigue and a wobbly gait. "I was devastated," remembers Ford, who now lives in Melbourne, Florida. "But then I decided to just let it play out."

The bond between Ford and Izzy, and the similarity between their diagnoses, caught

BLACK AND TAN COONHOUND

- ◆ ORIGIN: U.S.A.
- ◆ COLOR(S): Rich black with tan markings above the eyes; on the sides of the muzzle; and on the chest, legs, and rear end
- ◆ HEIGHT: 23 to 27 inches
- ◆ TEMPERAMENT: Outgoing, friendly, able to work with other dogs

was a subject that wasn't the most popular and might be hard to hear—but with Izzy there, people let their guards down and my message was able to get to their hearts. There's something about an animal being there that makes people more vulnerable."

Izzy defied the odds, living until she was almost ten years old, and Ford honors her by continuing to give antibullying talks across the country. "She wasn't trained, and she did have some bad manners when she was around other dogs, but she was my sidekick," says Ford. "As long as people hear my story she will [always] be alive, because she's the reason I have my story. There's the story of my being bullied—but the reason I was able to overcome my fears was because of her. She changed me. If it wasn't for her, I would still be a fearful person hiding away in my house." ◆

the attention of *Animal Planet*, and with the resulting segment that chronicles their story —which has aired more than 80 times over five years—came requests for the young woman to speak in classrooms about her experience of being bullied. "I was absolutely panicked, and there's no way I could have done it without Izzy," says Ford. "What made it OK was that all the attention went to her, which took the focus off me and my wheelchair. Everyone just loved her. Here

DOGS STAND UP TO BULLIES Mutt-i-grees, a program developed by Yale University and North Shore Animal League, uses some of the teachings of Cesar Millan and takes dogs in the classroom to teach children social and emotional skills, such as empathy, team building, and respect. The program has proved to be an effective tool in fighting bullying and is being introduced to more schools around the country.

Jarod

CHOW CHOW ◆ CANADA

Donna Perreault was accustomed to living in peace with her two chow chows—the breed is known to be fiercely protective—and the occasional bear who would amble across her land in Genelle, British Columbia. But one fall day as dusk fell, Perreault was on the phone with her son when she looked out the window and saw a dark figure moving toward her elderly female chow, Meesha, who was sleeping in the backyard.

Suddenly, Meesha began barking wildly, and then the bear was on top of the dog, attacking her.

"The wind had been blowing all day, and I think because of that the bear couldn't smell Meesha so he was startled when she barked," says Perreault. Without a thought, she threw the phone down and raced outside to try to distract the bear, only to find that her male chow, Jarod, had pushed the door open and raced after her. "Suddenly, he was attacking the bear, who was attacking Meesha," she remembers. "I had a mop bucket, so I picked it up and hit the bear on the butt, and that's when the bear came after me. He backed me up against the garage. I then hit him with the mop but he kept coming at me.

CHOW CHOWS are a favorite among the stars of screen and stage, with such famous owners as Sarah Bernhardt and Elvis Presley.

OPPOSITE: *Jarod, a chow chow, saved his owner and a canine companion from a brutal bear attack.*

CHOW CHOW

- ORIGIN: **China**
- COLOR(S): **Red, black, blue, cinnamon, and cream**
- HEIGHT: **17 to 20 inches**
- TEMPERAMENT: **Very loyal, intelligent, independent, naturally protective, reserved and discerning with strangers**

I whacked him on the nose and he stopped for a second and shook his head, and that's when Jarod attacked him."

Jarod went after the bear, forcing the animal to turn toward him and drawing the animal away from Perreault long enough for her and Meesha to race inside the house; Jarod followed shortly, with the bear nowhere in sight.

Remarkably, neither dog was seriously hurt—Meesha threw her back out—while Perreault suffered only puncture wounds to her hand from the bear clawing at her and a shallow wound in her chest that required some medical attention. (Perhaps the most frightened of all was Perreault's son, who had been on the phone the entire time listening to his mother scream.) "I think the bear just got caught up in the whole mess with us," says Perreault, who credits Jarod with saving her life as well as Meesha's. "Jarod was so happy to know we were all fine. Now, when we go on walks, he never lets me out of his sight." ◆

Jarod (left), Donna Perreault, and Meesha (right)

THE ORIGINAL TEDDY BEAR? Move over, Teddy Roosevelt. In the 1800s, England's Queen Victoria had a pet chow chow who was her constant companion. One legend states that the queen's dressmaker made a stuffed toy chow chow that some people thought looked like a bear. Other dressmakers followed suit, and the toys soon became known as teddy bears.

Picasso

Anyone in their right mind who is participating in a long-distance run enlists a partner to keep him or her motivated and on pace during the grueling and endless hours of training. And sometimes, if the athlete's very lucky, the partner will drag him or her up that final, seemingly insurmountable hill. ◆ Picasso does that for George Gallego, who became paraplegic two decades ago. The former manager of the *New York Times*'s circulation department for the tri-state area, Gallego tripped on a cable that had carelessly been left on the floor at work and plummeted from a three-story height, landing on a concrete floor. "My spinal cord was instantly severed," says Gallego, "and my life changed completely."

Gallego went on to earn a master's degree and professional certification in not-for-profit management. He then founded Wheels of Progress, a group dedicated to ensuring that thousands of young people currently living in senior nursing facilities because they have spinal cord injuries or other disabilities and their homes are no longer accessible have the chance to live in their own apartments again. He also began racing for the cause. And he found Picasso.

THE CHOICE of a canine running partner always depends on conditions such as local weather, temperament, and the dog's physical ability.

PAGE 103: *George Gallego and Picasso go for a run in Central Park in New York City.*

DOGS WHO GO THE DISTANCE

- Biskotouli, a rescue black-and-tan mixed breed, ran the 29th Athens Classic Marathon (26.2 miles) with his two running partners in under four hours.
- Xiao Sa, a stray mixed-breed dog, joined up with a biking troop and ran (and occasionally rode) more than 1,100 miles during a three-week trek across the Qinghai-Tibet Plateau.

"I never understood the phrase 'A dog is a man's best friend' until he entered my life," Gallego says. "When I first saw him, he was being abused by a three-year-old boy, who was hitting him across the nose with a stool. He was only six weeks old, and I approached the father of the child and offered to buy the puppy."

Gallego's wife, a marathon runner, began teaching Picasso how to accompany her husband while he runs in a push-rim racing chair. "She trained him to become a pacer," he explains, "since keeping a steady pace is important when training. Because he is a 'steady runner,' he encourages me to stay on point. He keeps me company when I am doing four- to six-hour training runs. There have been times, when I injured my shoulder and couldn't continue pushing uphill, when he has pulled me up and over the hill. He is so loyal and willing to please, how can a dog not be a man's best friend?"

In 2011, Gallego completed the NYC Triathlon, and in doing so raised enough money to move a 21-year-old from a senior nursing facility into an apartment.

For Gallego, Picasso's encouragement has made it possible to continue fighting for the rights of those less fortunate than he. "There are days when I may have left a nursing home in a depressed state, or just had a long day's work and feel like I have nothing left," he says. "But one look into his eyes and my worries are gone. All I see is a companion who only wants to be loved." ◆

IS YOUR DOG DESIGNED FOR DISTANCE? Some breeds are naturally suited for long-distance running, such as sled dogs or hunting dogs. Short-legged dogs are generally not suited for long distances; nor are squishy-nosed dogs, because they overheat easily.

Louise

▶ BEARDED COLLIE ◆ NEW YORK

In the maelstrom of downtown Manhattan on September 11, 2001, comfort was hard to come by. But on a triage boat that brought survivors from the ruins of the World Trade Center to New Jersey, a lost dog named Louise spent the day offering solace and distraction to the traumatized passengers. ◆ Louise, a bearded collie, was adopted at the age of four by Abby McGrath and her husband, who commuted between a country house

in upstate New York and an apartment in Manhattan. On September 11, they had driven down from Martha's Vineyard and had reached lower Manhattan when a piece of debris fell through their roof. "We pulled to the side of the road and got out and looked around, and the World Trade Center had smoke coming out of it and papers were flying everywhere, but there was dead silence. No sirens, nothing," remembers McGrath.

Then there was a big *boom,* and when McGrath looked back into the car Louise was gone—spooked by the noise.

There was only an instant to worry about the dog: The couple turned back and saw the second tower collapse. There was ash everywhere, black ash

AFTER THE 9/11 terrorist attacks, more than 300 search-and-rescue dogs were deployed to ground zero in New York City.

OPPOSITE: *Louise survived the 9/11 attacks in New York City and brought cheer to those stranded on Liberty Island.*

BEARDED COLLIE

- ORIGIN: **One of Britain's oldest breeds; probably originated with the komondor, a central European breed, but later used in Scotland for herding**
- COLOR(S): **Black, blue, brown, or fawn, with or without white markings**
- HEIGHT: **20 to 22 inches**
- TEMPERAMENT: **Active, strong, devoted dog with no signs of shyness or aggression, the bearded collie has been bred for centuries to be a companion.**

that filled the air and coated their faces. As panic filled the streets, they realized that their safest bet was to go to a nearby colleague's home.

They were waiting to hear news of Louise when a woman from Liberty Island called to say that the dog was safe, but that they couldn't pick her up until the island reopened to the public. Three days later, the phone rang and the McGraths were told they could come to the island. It was then, too,

that they learned of Louise's heroism by the side of a ferryboat captain named Chuck.

Chuck, seeing Louise running down the street in a panic, grabbed the end of her leash, assuming her owners would appear momentarily. By the time he realized that wasn't the case, "it was too late," says McGrath. "They were in the middle of black ash, their lungs filling up." Chuck and Louise ran to a yacht docked nearby, where Chuck—whose job was operating a ferryboat between New York and Martha's Vineyard—locked the two of them downstairs in the cabin to keep the ash out. Chuck then passed out, regaining consciousness as Louise licked his face. Hearing the ferry going by, he ran to ask whether they might get on.

"He was told it was a triage boat and there was no more room," McGrath remembers, "but he explained he was a captain who could help. They said he had to leave the dog, and he said no." So Louise and Chuck got onto the boat, where they spent the rest of that day helping as they could.

and Chuck said then they all started to smile." All day this went on, back and forth with new, terrified passengers. "She made them comfortable and happy and took their minds off the issues."

For the next three days, Captain Chuck and Louise lived in the makeshift shelter at Liberty Island until the island reopened to the public and the McGraths could pick up Louise. "When I got there, the people who were working there said, 'Please don't take Louise. She's the thing that keeps us going,'" McGrath remembers.

Louise at first refused to get back in the car, and disliked riding in it for much of the fall. Eventually, she seemed to forget the trauma; she died in 2010, at the age of 15. McGrath stayed in touch with Chuck until he decided that because of the trauma of September 11 he could no longer live in New York City. "We've had dogs who weren't perfect, but she was," says McGrath of Louise. "She was the dog of all dogs." ◆

Louise and family friend Isabel Powell on the beach

"All the kids and the people were petting her, and she was licking their faces," McGrath says. "She was comforting them

WHY DOGS LICK YOUR FACE Dogs' instinct to lick your face or other part of your body stems from their wolf ancestry, where licking is viewed as a form of communication. Puppies lick their mothers to let them know that they are hungry. Modern domesticated puppies might try to get some food from you by licking your face. Licking a person's face is a sign of respect and of the fact that the dog accepts the owner's leadership role.

Bear

MIXED BREED ◆ WASHINGTON, D.C.

Holly Barnes didn't go to Afghanistan looking for love. As a civilian employed by USAID, Barnes was supposed to embed with the military and to work with Afghans toward stabilizing communities in the war-torn region. ◆ In June 2011, after nearly four months of living in chaos without a single day off, Barnes booked herself to go to Amsterdam for a few days of leave. "I desperately needed to get away from the intensity to a place that was clean and safe," she says. But when she arrived at the airport, she was told she didn't have the proper paperwork to leave the country. So it was back to work, this time on assignment in southern Afghanistan, an area she describes as "fairly kinetic," but relatively safe compared with where she had most recently been stationed, as it had been cleared and held by the U.S. Marines for several months.

Two plane rides and two helicopter rides later, an exhausted Barnes, still disappointed not to have had a break, arrived at a forward operating base in southern Afghanistan on a day so hot that there were reports that the asphalt on the street was melting. When she was led into a cool tent she felt her

SERGEANT STUBBY, a stray mixed breed, was the most decorated dog in World War I history and the first dog to be given a rank in the U.S. armed forces.

OPPOSITE: *Holly Barnes and Bear share a hug.*

DOGS ON THE BATTLEFIELD

- Cairo, a Belgian Malinois, became famous for his role in the top-secret mission to capture or kill Osama bin Laden in May 2011.
- Dogs' superior sense of smell is prized by the military. After four years and billions of dollars in research to establish a technology to locate an improvised explosive device (IED), the Pentagon admitted that no technology was better for this task than a dog's nose.
- The United States had 2,800 dogs deployed worldwide in 2011, more than any other country.

heart lift at a surprising sight: a mother dog and her two six-month-old puppies. The Marines introduced Barnes to Claire, an Afghan mixed breed they had found on the side of the road and taken into the compound along with her offspring, Bear and Dozer. Another dog, named Jack, was also living on the base. The dogs accompanied the men on patrol and were rewarded with leftover rations at mealtime.

Barnes was immediately smitten: "I've never seen a dog more loving than Bear," she says. During the day, "I would go into the tent where they lived more than I needed to, and I think the Marines thought I was nuts. They were all so proper and professional and I would sit on the floor with Bear's head on my lap while we were having briefing meetings." After about two weeks, Bear followed her into her room and lay down.

The Marines felt just as strongly about the canine clan. But while having the dogs was an enormous comfort, it was also against the rules. "These dogs were clearly a morale boost for them, but there is something called General Order Number One, which states that on base there is . . . no alcohol, and no pets," says Barnes. Taking stray dogs into military bases not only can prove distracting but also can put the personnel at risk for rabies.

Three weeks after Barnes arrived, her short assignment came to an end. On the day of her departure, she knelt down before Bear. "I told him I didn't know how or when, but I would claim him as mine one day. I had no idea how I could make that a reality, but I promised

Bear made the long journey from Afghanistan to the United States to be reunited with Barnes.

him, myself, and the Marines who loved him that I would find a way. I am sure about few things," she continues, "but something about Bear convinced me it was my privilege and obligation to make sure he would be safe."

Three months later, when she was in Kandahar, Barnes received an email asking her to make good on her promise: An incoming commanding officer had ordered the men to get rid of the dogs. In short order, they would be put down. But if Barnes could help, the men would try to buy time.

Barnes found the Nowzad shelter in Kabul, founded by a British Royal Marine, which agreed to care for the dogs provided their transportation could be arranged. A sergeant

Barnes with Jack (left) and Bear (right) on the day of their arrival in Houston, Texas

agreed to escort them by helicopter for what would be a three-day journey. The animals arrived safely, but getting them out of the country and providing proper health care would cost several thousand dollars per dog.

The mother, Claire, had bonded with a major who had since returned to the States. At the Marines' suggestion, Barnes got in touch with her; immediately, the major arranged for Claire—who was pregnant—to fly to her home in North Carolina. That left Bear and his buddy Jack (Dozer, Bear's brother, had shown signs of aggression, according to the Marines, and been put down.) "I paid $5,000 of my own money, and I still hadn't met my mark," says Barnes. "And the shelter was getting concerned about the expense in caring for the two dogs, Bear in particular, who at about a year old weighed some 90 pounds and was roughly the size of a Great Dane."

Barnes turned to friends and family but couldn't meet the goal. A generous couple in Texas, hearing of her plight from the Soldiers' Animal Companions Fund, made up the difference; on April 6, Bear and Jack boarded a flight to Houston, Texas. Barnes, who had returned from Afghanistan just a few days before, was at the airport to greet them, along with Jack's adopter, a friend of Barnes's from Austin. Also there were the donors who had made it all possible, who drove from Dallas to videotape the event. "Then we learned customs had to sign off before we could take possession of the dogs, and I panicked. It was 4:43 p.m. on the Thursday before Easter weekend," Barnes remembers. "But I raced over there and just told them the story, and they stamped the paperwork."

Now, Bear and Barnes have settled into their new apartment outside Washington, D.C., where both are recovering from life in a war zone. "He still cowers at loud noises," says Barnes. "We both do. But he's ridiculously happy and getting more confident every day. He frolics in the park with other dogs, and he's so gentle with them." At night, he sleeps soundly beside her. As for Barnes, "When I was in Afghanistan, I was just focused on getting through the day. Coming back was difficult. Reconnecting with people was surprisingly hard. I don't know what I would do without Bear. The best part of each day is the part with Bear. We are meant to be together." ◆

> I don't know what I would do without Bear. The best part of each day is the part with Bear.

WHY ARE CERTAIN DOGS SUITED FOR WAR? Bear may not have been on the battlefield, but many dogs do serve in the armed forces. The German shepherd and Belgian Malinois are the most common breeds used by the military. Some characteristics of these well-suited war dogs include a sharp sense of smell, courage, intelligence, adaptability, strength, and speed.

Cooper

GERMAN SHORTHAIRED POINTER ◆ KENTUCKY

Dogs who are owned for the purpose of performing a specific task—herding sheep, for instance—are often viewed more as valued workers than as pets. Then there is Cooper, a German shorthaired pointer who was raised from puppyhood by Mike Cole to retrieve pheasants, ducks, and quail. ◆ Cooper proved to be preternaturally adept at the task. By the age of four months, he was pointing, and shortly thereafter he was bounding after the fallen creatures and retrieving them for his owner with extraordinary precision. When he senses a bird nearby, "he crouches like a tiger, moves slow as the scent is coming in, and as the scent comes in strong he will not move," says Cole. "He's getting high on that bird scent. It's a buzz to him."

For two years, Cooper was Cole's constant companion, traveling from their home in Mount Sterling, Kentucky, to hunt in Nebraska, Minnesota, and Wisconsin. At night, he would sleep at the foot of his master's bed. Says Cole, "There's a bond between hunter and hunting dog that can't be explained."

And then, when Cooper was two years old, he was

THE POINTER is one of the five oldest breeds of hunting dogs along with sheepherding dogs, mastiffs, greyhounds, and wolf hybrids.

OPPOSITE: *Cooper, a German shorthaired pointer, lost the sight in both eyes at the age of two.*

- ORIGIN: **Thought to be Germany**
- COLOR(S): **Solid liver or combination of liver and white**
- HEIGHT: **21 to 25 inches**
- TEMPERAMENT: **Friendly, intelligent, willing to please, and enthusiastic**

sprayed in the face by a skunk while hunting. The next day, when Cole checked on Cooper's face, he noticed that something about the dog's eyes looked off. A visit to the vet brought crushing news: Cooper had blastomycosis, a disease caused by a fungus that can result in blindness. One of his eyes had to be removed, and he lost sight in the other. The vet, knowing what often happens to hunting dogs who are no longer able to do their jobs, asked whether Cole wanted to keep his dog alive. When Cole said there was no other option, the vet smiled and said, "That's all I needed to hear."

Then one day Cooper fell off the porch. "I was sitting there bawling," Cole remembers. "I was thinking, 'This isn't fair to him. I'm keeping him alive because I can't deal with putting him down.' " Cole told his wife what he was thinking, and she replied, 'Good. Now we know what to do about you if you go blind.' " And that, says Cole, was that. "Cooper the bird dog might be over," Cole remembers deciding, "but Cooper my best friend will have a long life. He's my best friend, and this is between him and me."

Over the next four months, Cooper and Cole made some ten trips to a vet in Cincinnati to treat Cooper. "I went in one time and there was a young woman in there and I asked her if she was OK and she said, 'My dog is going to be blind.' I said, 'It's not that bad.' I went to my truck and got Cooper," who hopped down without a leash, tail wagging, to greet them. "And I told her he was blind. She was surprised, but I told her, 'You'll be closer than you've ever been. You'll be his Seeing Eye human.' "

When Cooper first lost his sight, Cole imagined that he would only be a house dog, but he has continued to keep Cole company on all his trips. Not only does he still

Cooper and Mike Cole still enjoy the outdoors together.

go hunting, he accompanies Cole when he gives presentations explaining bird hunting to children. "Cooper doesn't know he is blind, and his hearing and smelling capabilities are phenomenal," says Cole. "And he is so smart. I can be feeling down and he'll do something silly. I'd rather get one bird with him than five with my other dogs. It's not about the numbers but about quality time. It's about friends." ◆

HOW LONG HAVE HUMANS USED DOGS FOR HUNTING? The origin of the hunting dog dates back thousands of years, to when a hunter's life depended on his hunting success. Hunters used dogs to help hunt for food and hides for clothing. The hunting dog's role changed as humans started to breed dogs for specialized roles such as guarding and companionship.

Alfie

MIXED BREED ◆ OHIO

As the activities director at Victoria House Assisted Living facility in Austintown, Ohio, Susan Greco is supposed to come up with ways to brighten the residents' lives. Perhaps her most inspired idea was to open up the home not just to the occasional dog visitor but to a dog-in-residence. ◆ Concerned that a puppy would prove to be too difficult to raise properly, Greco contacted Close to Home Animal Rescue on a recommendation from her sister-in-law. The group was beginning a pilot program that would bring dogs into nursing homes. Close to Home Animal Rescue introduced Greco to three different dogs, but ultimately it was Alfie, an older yellow Labrador retriever mix who had been rescued from a shelter just a few days before she was to be euthanized, who immediately won everyone over. "She wasn't trained as a therapy dog, but she was a great dog. She approached three residents and let them love on her," remembers Greco. "And it was like she had always been there."

Despite her lack of formal training, Alfie—or Miss Alfie, as the residents fondly refer to her—has

> THERAPY DOGS INTERNATIONAL, founded in 1976, is the oldest registry of therapy dogs in the United States.

OPPOSITE: *Alfie visits with some of the residents of Victoria House Assisted Living facility.*

Alfie is a constant companion to the residents and employees.

nursing station; by day, she wanders the facility, making rounds. "She has many roles here. She will go into the beauty salon and lie there while people are having their hair done. People said we would have trouble getting people taking her out, but residents fight over walking her. We have one lady who has a little depression problem but if she's having a bad day she will sit with Miss Alfie and talk to her, and it helps. She plays with people's grandchildren and other dogs if a visitor brings one. She is everything everyone needs her to be."

With more than 5 million people currently suffering from dementia—which is a number expected to reach upwards of 15 million by 2050—researchers have been spurred to discover new ways to alleviate the effects of the disease, which is marked by the gradual deterioration of mental functioning. Top of the treatment list is animal therapy. One study, published by the *American Journal of Alzheimer's Disease and Other Dementias,* involved 56 nursing home residents with dementia who were asked to interact with real dogs, a robotic dog, a puppy video, and a stuffed dog. The study's conclusion: "Nursing homes should consider animal-assisted therapy and dog-related

behaved perfectly from the start. "The only thing she had a bit of hesitancy about was the residents in wheelchairs, but we worked with her on that and she's great," says Greco. At night, Alfie retires to her bed at the 24-hour

DOGS HELPING OTHERS

- Smoky, a four-pound Yorkshire terrier, is recognized as the first therapy dog because of her service comforting wounded soldiers in the 233rd Station Hospital in New Guinea during World War II.
- In 2011, the American Kennel Club created the AKC Therapy Dog Program honoring dogs who are working in the field in order to advance the work of visiting therapy dogs and other experts in the field. In July 2011, the AKC bestowed the first "Th.D." titles on six dogs who have helped improve people's lives. The dogs were recognized for their community service and the help they provide to improve the well-being of others.

stimuli, as they successfully engage residents with dementia."

Risë VanFleet, Ph.D., a child and family psychologist who has helped develop the field of animal-assisted play therapy, which integrates interaction with animals into therapy sessions, says having a dog on the premises of nursing homes helps in more ways than just the obvious benefit of added affection. "I've seen examples where two older people might have the same conversation day after day, and all of a sudden a dog comes in and they are interacting with each other and sharing smiles in a totally different way. The dog has a social lubricant effect, which is really important for people who are living more socially isolated lives."

At Victoria House, Alfie works her magic every day. "Everyone is involved in her well-being. She tore her ACL and we had to take her to the emergency room. We probably had 20 residents sitting on the front porch when she returned, waiting to make sure she was OK," says Greco. "We often say she was placed here for a reason, because she has truly been a blessing. She has made a difference in all of our lives." ◆

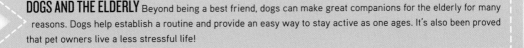

DOGS AND THE ELDERLY Beyond being a best friend, dogs can make great companions for the elderly for many reasons. Dogs help establish a routine and provide an easy way to stay active as one ages. It's also been proved that pet owners live a less stressful life!

Casey

SHETLAND SHEEPDOG ♦ OKLAHOMA

It took two days for Kristin Kelly to persuade the starving, terrified sheltie to leave the side of the road where he had been abandoned. With a boot-mark–shaped bruise on his belly, and with matted fur, the dog was in terrible shape, but despite the freezing cold and his obvious need for nourishment, he at first refused to be won over by treats. ♦ After two days, Kelly was able to coax Casey, as the sheltie became known, into their home, where he charmed not only Kristin's husband but her mother-in-law, Oleta, who begged that Casey be allowed to live with her. For more than four years, the two cohabited with joy. Oleta would share half of her Meals on Wheels food with Casey, and Casey shared all his love in return. But after a debilitating stroke, Oleta had to move to a nursing home 11 miles away. Casey went back to live with the Kellys but frequently visited Oleta.

Then the Kellys went away for a week, leaving Casey in the care of a man who worked on their farm. One day, "he called and said, 'Your mother's dog has disappeared,'" Kelly remembers. The region happened to be suffering a historic drought, with temperatures reaching

DOGS USE their sense of smell to understand the world. The area of a dog's brain dedicated to registering smells is proportionally 40 times the size of the same area in a human brain.

OPPOSITE: *Casey, a Shetland sheepdog, was rescued from the side of the road.*

SHETLAND SHEEPDOG

- ◆ ORIGIN: **Shetland Islands, Scotland**
- ◆ COLOR(S): **Black, blue merle, and sable; marked with varying amounts of white and/or tan**
- ◆ HEIGHT: **Between 13 and 16 inches**
- ◆ TEMPERAMENT: **Intensely loyal, affectionate, and responsive to his owner**

---

115 degrees every day, and Casey was missing for five weeks. "We thought he was dead."

And then, all of a sudden, he appeared—at the nursing home. Casey had lost half his body weight, but there he was, having sought out his owner through the worst conditions. A nurse's aide later said that she had seen the dog at the back door of the home for a couple of days, but hadn't realized it was the once healthy Casey.

"A dog's ability to recognize where it is through scent is extraordinary," says canine expert and trainer Philip Levine. "It is not beyond the intellectual capacity of a dog to take inventory of what's around him. It's the equivalent of you or me driving somewhere and looking here and there, but a dog is doing it with odors. Take a dog out of a familiar place within a 100-mile radius, and it's very, very easy for a dog to find his way home."

So what about pets who, unlike Casey, aren't able to find their way back to their families? Assuming someone like an animal control officer hasn't interrupted their journey, says Levine, the cause is generally stress: "A dog's emotional, frenetic state influences their decision making the same way it influences ours," he explains. "Most dogs in emotional upset will pant, which oxygenates the brain. The dog is hyperventilating, so like a person, it can get loopy. A calmer dog will be able to find its way home easier than a dog in an agitated state."

The only panting Casey is doing these days is while he chases the UPS driver. Oleta has since passed away, but before she died she said, "I've had a good life." And a very good dog. ◆

HAVEN'T I HEARD THIS STORY BEFORE? This might sound familiar to those who've read *The Incredible Journey*. Sheila Burnford's book chronicles the journey of three pets who try to find their way home to their owners, who they mistakenly think have abandoned them.

Wang Cai

POMERANIAN ◆ CHINA

Waiting in line at the bank ranks up there with life's more tedious tasks. But imagine waiting *outside* the bank . . . for eight hours. That's what Wang Cai, a Pomeranian mix in Chongqing, China, has done every day for four years, spending his days watching the world go by while his owner works nearby. ◆ When footage of Wang Cai's typical day hit the Internet, it went viral, logging more than 1.3 million views in 24 hours on China's video-hosting service Youku .com. Dressed in a snazzy red and black coat, the petite Wang Cai greets passersby with charm—other dogs get chased away—but rarely leaves his sentry post on the steps of the Minsheng bank.

Wang Cai was found wandering the streets; his loyalty to his adopter and savior has drawn comparisons to Hachikó, an Akita in Japan who became famous for his devotion to his owner, a professor at the University of Tokyo. Every day, the dog greeted his owner at the Shibuya train station at the end of the day. When the owner died suddenly, the dog continued his daily trips to the station, appearing precisely as the scheduled train arrived, for the next nine years of his life. The story of the Akita made

IN SHANGHAI, China's most dog-friendly city, 140,000 dogs are registered as pets.

NEXT PAGE: *Wang Cai loyally waits outside the bank where his owner works.*

POMERANIAN

- ORIGIN: **From Pomerania (now Germany and Poland), the dog was developed from the ancient spitz**
- COLOR(S): **All colors**
- HEIGHT: **7 to 12 inches**
- TEMPERAMENT: **Friendly, intelligent, active; companion or competitive show dog**

are creatures of survival, and identify a person who is benevolent, who provides food, shelter, and identification," he explains. "They are also creatures of contextualized awareness, and if something works for them, they will repeat it. And this dog has a good thing going." Not to mention an ever growing fan club. ◆

such an impression on the country that the dog's remains are stuffed and mounted at the National Science Museum of Japan in Tokyo, and every year on April 8 there is a solemn ceremony in his honor held at the Shibuya train station.

Wang Cai's owner has said that she neither asked nor trained the dog to wait for her. Canine expert and trainer Philip Levine isn't surprised Wang Cai does so anyway—and says it isn't necessarily just about love. "Dogs

Hachikō was another famously loyal dog.

LIKE CLOCKWORK It's a familiar scene to a dog owner: Your dog is waiting at the door when you arrive home from work. How do they know? Dogs have an incredible ability to pick up on small environmental clues and sounds we humans don't notice. Although there is a lack of hard-hitting science, it is believed that dogs may even recognize the sound of your car's engine or the bus that you take home from work, alerting them to your impending arrival.

Hattie

H attie does all the things a dog for the deaf is supposed to: She alerts her owner, Jennifer Warsing Hampton, when the doorbell rings; she leads her to the phone when someone is calling; she nudges her when the oven timer goes off. But the chocolate Lab has also warned Hampton of an imminent earthquake, led her to crying children in the playground, and nosed her owner before pointing skyward so she might see migrating geese.

"She 'alerts' to everything," says Hattie's trainer, Carrie Brooks of Dogs for the Deaf. "There are dogs who just do extraordinary things that you could not imagine."

Before Hattie, Hampton says she lived "the life of a hermit." Dependent upon a flashing device that let her know someone had arrived at the house, Hampton didn't order deliveries, since waiting for them entailed standing at the door endlessly until they arrived. She loved cooking but burned endless meals because she couldn't hear the timer going off. More stressful were the dangers of living alone as a deaf woman: "I had sleepless nights where I didn't feel safe in my own home. What if there was a power outage and my smoke detector failed to alert me?" Hampton says. "During

NEADS, the oldest hearing dog program in the United States, has trained more than 1,300 dogs since its founding in 1976.

OPPOSITE: *Hattie and Jennifer Warsing Hampton share an embrace.*

ALL ABOUT HEARING DOGS

- Hearing dogs are trained to alert to household sounds that ensure everyday safety and self-sufficiency for their owner.
- There is not one specific breed best suited to be a hearing dog. Most hearing dogs are mixed breeds, and dogs suited to the work tend to have a high energy level.

the day, I felt like I was walking on eggshells. I hated being at home, but I stayed inside because what was the point in going beyond my front door when I had no idea what was going on around me?"

But life with Hattie is filled with endless possibilities. "After Hattie's arrival I cooked an entire Thanksgiving meal for my family, and I have done one every year since," says Hampton. "Hattie is my ears who can alert me to the kitchen timer going off while I am doing other things. I have been able to bake dozens of Christmas cookies to give out as gifts, something I wouldn't have even attempted before Hattie."

Hattie also instinctively anticipates any possible harm. One day, Hattie kept poking Hampton while she was at the computer. Unable to figure out what she was alerting her to, Hampton continued to work. Suddenly, Hattie pushed her body against Hampton's chair and pinned her against the desk so she was unable to get up. "As soon as she did that, I felt a strange rolling sensation as if the ground were making waves under me," Hampton remembers. "When I returned to the computer I discovered that we had just experienced aftershocks in Pennsylvania from the earthquake that hit Virginia [in 2011]."

Thanks to Hattie's companionship, Hampton has been spending less time at the desk where she drafted "Hattie's Law," a bill that protects the rights of service dogs from attacks by other dogs in Pennsylvania. Advocating for the passage of this law was important to Hampton because Hattie had previously been attacked by another dog. "Before Hattie, rather than coming right out and saying, 'I'm deaf,' . . . if I didn't hear something someone said, I would just nod in agreement, with no clue to what I

Hattie in Portstown Park in Huntingdon, Pennsylvania

was agreeing to," remembers Hampton. "With Hattie in my life, I no longer hide behind my deafness." The one caveat for people in her life? "You know that phrase 'Love me, love my dog?' That's true for me and then some," says Hampton. "She's actually helped me discover who the true friends are in my life."

Not to mention helped Hampton identify her true love—second to Hattie, of course. "The day my husband, Chris, proposed, he asked Hattie's permission first. He leaned down and whispered into Hattie's ear. I saw Hattie's tail wag and the next thing I know Hattie lets out this belting *Awrrrooooo!!!!!*, Hampton remembers. "Chris turned around to me with a smile across his face and said, 'Hattie said yes!' And then he asked me to marry him. We are all a match made in heaven." ◆

HATTIE'S LAW Hattie serves as the icon and namesake of legislation passed in Pennsylvania that protects service/assistance animals and their users against aggressive attacks from other dogs. This is the first law of its kind passed in the United States.

Lilly

PIT BULL ◆ MASSACHUSETTS

Lilly didn't just take a hit for her owner; she took on an oncoming train. Rescued from a Boston shelter by David Lanteigne, a police officer, Lilly, a pit bull, seemed to have all the qualities he thought would make the perfect companion for his mother, who struggles with depression and alcoholism. "Lilly seemed shy and nervous and tired all rolled into one," Lanteigne remembers, "and then she pushed herself up against the bars to be pet. I took her for a walk and she got so excited and her tail started wagging. And she had the most beautiful eyes. She was magical."

Lanteigne asked his mother to come meet her. The three of them went for a walk, at the end of which, Lanteigne remembers, "I opened the trunk of my car, where I had treats for my own dog, in order to give her one, and Lilly jumped in the trunk like, 'Get me out of here.' I've never seen anything like it. She wanted to come home." And so she did.

For more than three years, Lilly was the center of Lanteigne's mother's universe. "She improved the quality of her life so much," he says. "She gave her a reason to get up in the morning. Lilly is the nicest, sweetest, funniest

PIT BULLS on U.S. military posters during World War I were often referred to as "the American Watch Dog."

OPPOSITE: *Lilly visits the Littleton Animal Hospital in June 2012.*

133

- As relatives to wolves and distant relatives to other pack animals, dogs continue to be a pack-oriented species.
- When dogs feel a part of the pack, they can be protective of the pack or owner, which is why they make great guards and service companions.
- If you want your dog to be part of the family pack, keep your dog in the house rather than outside. This will strengthen the bond between you and your dog.

dog, with this giant, wonderful smile. There's no one who doesn't love Lilly."

Lanteigne says that having Lilly helped his mother continue her sobriety. But then, one night, she met a friend after hearing some upsetting news, and one drink turned to many. As she was walking home with Lilly by her side, she stumbled across the train tracks and slipped, unable to get up. A train was bearing down.

"The conductor said he could see a mass, and as he got closer he could see that this mass was a woman and a dog," says Lanteigne. "And then he saw the dog trying to pull the woman off the tracks. He went to tell someone to stop the train, and then he went back to the window and saw that the dog had circled up to the woman's head to stand between the train and the person. He told me, 'That dog intentionally took the hit for your mom.'"

When the conductor ran onto the tracks, "He saw my mother on the ground and the dog was lying next to her, unable to move." But as help arrived, Lilly, despite her injuries, continued to crawl across the ground to put herself between her owner and the first responders. "The conductor said there wasn't one sign of aggression, but she just kept repositioning herself to make sure my mom was OK."

Lanteigne quickly went to be with Lilly, visiting while she was in the hospital for weeks. The leg that was run over by the train had to be amputated, and a later surgery mended Lilly's fractured pelvis and her rear left leg, which is now supported with steel plates. But she was alive. "I've been through a lot in my life," says Lanteigne. "And in my job I work murders and stabbings and shootings and

Lilly saved the life of David Lanteigne's mother by pulling her out of the path of an oncoming train.

I'm fine. But I had never been so devastated in my entire life as when Lilly got hurt."

As news of Lilly's heroics got out, strangers flooded the hospital with more than $76,000 in donations to help cover the cost of Lilly's veterinary treatment and physical therapy. Inspired by the outreach and support he received, Lanteigne founded Lilly's Fund, which raises money to help improve the quality of life for pit bulls in shelters. Lilly does her part by attending events to promote her breed. "When people meet her, it's not 'That's a scary pit bull,' but 'What a sweet, sweet dog,' " says Lanteigne. "She's absolutely inspiring." ◆

LILLY'S FUND Inspired by Lilly's heroic act, her family started Lilly's Fund to heighten awareness about the pit bull breed and their positive attributes and characteristics. Lilly's Fund raises money to support responsible dog ownership, adoption of pit bulls from shelters, and the repeal of breed-specific laws.

Rocky

MIXED BREED ◆ CALIFORNIA

When Rocky, a yellow Lab mix, arrived as a stray at the Lassen County Animal Shelter in California, the staff knew that the petrified dog stood no chance of being adopted. With bullets in his hip, a case of worms, and a terror of people, Rocky was destined to be euthanized. ◆ Then, at the last minute, he was rescued by Pups on Parole, a program that pairs traumatized and abused homeless dogs, who would otherwise be put to sleep, with prison inmates entrusted to socialize the dogs so they might be adopted. And so Rocky found himself in the care of the residents at the California Correctional Center, a state prison in Susanville, California. The inmates knew they were saving Rocky's life, but they would never have guessed Rocky would end up being a lifesaver himself.

In February 2011, Dawn Tibbetts, the secretary to the prison's captain, saw Rocky's picture in the facility's newsletter and thought she had found the perfect dog to accompany her husband, who'd retired from working at the correctional center, on his rock hunts. Floyd Tibbetts's hobby—searching for petrified wood, gems, gold, and special stones—involves long days in the Lassen National Forest, which is populated by

THERE ARE 78.2 MILLION owned dogs in the United States.

OPPOSITE: *Rocky, a Lab mix, was rescued and later trained by prisoners in the California Correctional Center.*

- Dogs are rescued from shelters and trained in prison; they're made available for adoption after they complete the Pups on Parole program.
- Dog-training programs in various states have been shown to have significant rehabilitative effects on prisoners. Overall, the programs help to improve discipline and socialization skills and so help the prisoners become potentially productive citizens.
- Prison dog-training programs exist in many forms throughout the United States—service-dog training, police dog training, and general training for potential adoption.

mountain lions, bears, and coyotes. "There are dangers, and I didn't like him going out there by himself," says Dawn, "so I went to see Rocky. He was skittish and just wanted to go home with me. I went to my husband and said, 'Guess what? We have a new member of our family.'"

Although it took Rocky some time to adjust, Floyd was immediately smitten. He went out and bought a new truck that had room for Rocky to have his own seat in the crew cab, and began taking the dog out on his hunts with him. Then, in July 2011, only five months after the Tibbettses adopted Rocky, Floyd set off with him for an hour of rock hunting at 9:30 a.m. When they weren't home by 5 p.m., Dawn was in a panic.

She called her son, who went in search of him. At 7:30, as she called 911 for a search and rescue, Floyd pulled into the driveway. "He was so delirious he left the back wheels in the middle of the street. He was so weak he couldn't stand up. He wasn't making any sense. He was bloody. I said, 'I don't understand how you drove home,' and he said, 'I don't know if I drove home or if Rocky did.'"

Floyd's heart rate was dangerously low. An ambulance transported him to a hospital almost 90 miles away, in Reno, Nevada, where he received a pacemaker. Only then was he able to tell the story of how Rocky had saved his life.

After arriving at the site to look for rocks, Floyd and Rocky began hiking. Then, "I got and licked my hand. He stayed right there with me." For seven and a half hours, Rocky remained by Floyd's side, curled up next to him and licking him, until he was able to struggle up and start making his way back toward the truck. But Rocky refused to go with him. "I thought, 'Rocky, I don't need this,'" Floyd remembers. But Floyd slowly realized he was so disoriented he was walking in the wrong direction. He turned around and allowed Rocky to lead him back to the safety of the truck.

Once Floyd was safely back home, one of Dawn's first calls was to the Pups on Parole program. They helped find the inmate— who has since been released from prison— who was primarily responsible for Rocky's rehabilitation. "I got to tell him, and he was very proud," says Dawn. As for Rocky, he is still riding shotgun with Floyd when they go off hunting for treasures. "He's the most loving and affectionate dog I have ever had," says Dawn, "so this has been a blessing for him, too." ◆

Rocky and Floyd Tibbetts

violently ill, fell into the bushes, and lost my glasses," remembers Floyd, who had suffered from heart ailments in the past, although none life threatening. "Rocky just stayed

DOING HARD TIME On August 12, 1924, Pep, a black Labrador retriever, was sentenced to life without parole for killing a cat who belonged to the wife of Pennsylvania's governor, Gifford Pinchot. The governor, on the other hand, claimed that Pep had been sent to act as a mascot for the prisoners.

K'os

NEAPOLITAN MASTIFF ◆ CANADA

The Guindon family agrees that K'os (pronounced chaos), a Neapolitan mastiff, is patriarch Jason's dog. The two of them go everywhere together by day, and at night, K'os chooses to sleep on Jason's side of the bed. But K'os doesn't slumber for long: It turns out that much of his night is spent checking in on the Guindons' teenage son, Hunter. ◆ The Ontario, Canada, family wasn't aware of the dog's ritual until the parents were awakened in the middle of the night by the normally placid K'os barking furiously at them. While Jason ran downstairs to see if there was an intruder, Linda followed K'os into her son's room, where she discovered Hunter having a grand mal seizure. As she called an ambulance, K'os lay down beside Hunter to comfort him, remaining there until the paramedics took him to the hospital. Says Jason, "I only remember going to bed that night and waking up with the paramedics standing over me and K'os lying beside me."

When Hunter suffered another seizure just a few months later, K'os again alerted his parents. Hunter is no longer surprised by Kos's visits: "I can hear him come in all the time at

MASTIFFS FOUGHT against lions, tigers, bulls, bears, and human gladiators in the Colosseum in ancient Rome.

OPPOSITE: *K'os and Hunter Guindon pose for a picture after K'os's induction into the Purina Animal Hall of Fame.*

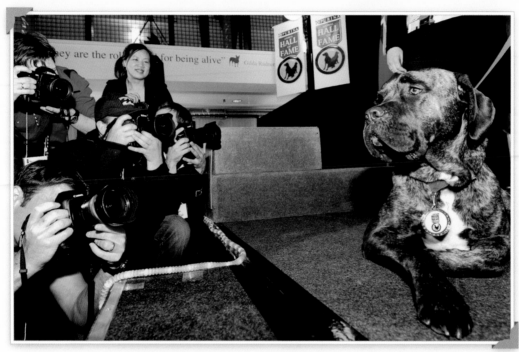

K'os was inducted into the Purina Animal Hall of Fame in Toronto in 2011.

night. Sometimes I will see him poke the door open and check on me." Adds Jason, "K'os normally sleeps on our bed, but several times a night I will hear him go down the hall, check in on Hunter, and then come back." Hunter, who was subsequently diagnosed with epilepsy, has since undergone brain surgery and is now seizure free.

Frank Petito, M.D., a neurologist at Cornell University, explains that a grand mal seizure would be easy for an alert dog to recognize as something amiss. "For starters, it causes breathing to become louder and more rapid," he says, "and then the arms and legs jerk dramatically. A patient will then stop breathing and stiffen and turn blue," which,

NEAPOLITAN MASTIFF

- ◆ ORIGIN: **An ancient breed from Egypt, Persia, Mesopo-tamia, and Asia, used by the Roman army**
- ◆ COLOR(S): **Solid gray (blue), black, mahogany, and tawny**
- ◆ HEIGHT: **24 to 31 inches**
- ◆ TEMPERAMENT: **Loyal, protective, watchful, calm, and steady**

while terrifying, is actually a sign that the seizure is about to subside. "The body self-corrects," says Petito, "with the cells that are firing electrically in the brain returning to normal."

"A grand mal seizure is physiologically dramatic," agrees dog expert and trainer Philip Levine, "and given that 80 percent of a dog's consciousness is about odor, it's something they would be very aware of." Levine, who is diabetic, points to the ability of his German shepherd to detect when his blood sugar is too low before he himself is aware of it. "She sits in front of me panting very heavily. The first time it happened I kept saying, 'What?' and then, a few minutes later, I was on the floor. Now I know that when she does it I need to go test my levels—and she's always right."

Owners looking for a supersensitive dog needn't run out and adopt a Neapolitan mastiff or German shepherd. Says Levine of K'os's devotion and care, "This isn't a breed-specific affair. This is a good-dog affair. K'os is extraordinarily generous in terms of his concern and service to his family." Says Jason Guindon of his son's savior, "I named him K'os because I had thought a large dog would put a little excitement in our lives. Instead, he has brought a calm, comforting peacefulness to our family. He's literally everyone's best friend. He's simply perfect." ◆

WHY DO DOGS BARK? Barking is most likely a result of domestication. It's commonplace among domesticated dogs but rare among wolves and other wild dogs, which howl and yip. Barking is seen as a warning signal for humans, who are able to distinguish certain types of barking—for example, alerting to a problem, or welcoming you home.

Dingo

MIXED BREED ◆ SOUTH CAROLINA

Friends of John Batchelor waved to him as they sailed past him and his boat *Joy B,* which was anchored at Memory Rock in the Bahamas. Batchelor, a Canadian, was a seasoned cruiser, so there was no need to worry about him, despite his decision to pause at the navigational rock favored by drug runners and modern-day pirates for its proximity to Florida and the Bahamas. But three weeks later, when the couple passed by again and saw the boat in the same spot, they called for help.

Nathan Moody, a volunteer with the Bahamas Air Sea Rescue Association, boarded the boat to find a disaster: The boat had been ransacked. Furniture and clothing were strewn about the cabin. Batchelor was nowhere to be found. But there, buried beneath rubble, lay his beloved dog Dingo. With protruding ribs and a deep gash in his hind leg, Dingo had managed to survive without food, water, or his companion. "I thought he was dead," remembers Moody. "His left eyeball was out of its socket because he was so dehydrated, but I checked his pulse and he was breathing."

But Dingo was too weak to walk. Moody carried the dog to his

THREE OF THE 12 DOGS aboard the R.M.S. *Titanic* survived the ship's sinking and were remembered in a centennial museum exhibit in 2012.

OPPOSITE: *A younger Dingo aboard the* Joy B

DOGS WITH SEA LEGS

- Senator Edward M. Kennedy and Splash, a Portuguese water dog, sailed together off the shores of Cape Cod, Massachusetts.
- President Franklin D. Roosevelt's Fala, a Scottish terrier, was a constant sailing companion, and even went on voyages as far as the West Indies.
- Sinbad, the world-famous U.S. Coast Guard mascot, was a mixed breed who sailed aboard the cutter *Campbell* during World War II and served for 11 years.

boat and rushed him 18 miles to the marina, then to an animal hospital in Freeport, Grand Bahama Island. With Batchelor presumed dead, the sailor's friends—who spoke of the dog and his owner's mutual adoration for each other—set up a fund to pay Dingo's veterinary bills, and put out feelers to see who might be able to adopt the dog when he had recovered.

Meanwhile, while Dingo lay in the vet's office on an IV drip, Nathan Moody began to fall in love with the 12-year-old Lab-greyhound mix. "He connects to people right off the bat," says Moody's brother, Rob. "He looks at you with an adorable face, he respects your space, and he does what he's told. If anyone has earned the right to live, it's Dingo." Nathan spoke up and said Dingo had found an adopter in the Bahamas—him.

At his new home, Dingo settled in immediately. "I have a pit bull named Ziggy who is very mothering to him," says Nathan, "and she sat beside him the whole time he recovered."

But Dingo's luck hadn't changed immediately: A few months after he went to live with Moody and Ziggy, they were attacked by a pack of stray dogs and he was severely wounded, with a resulting infection in his foot. That's when Rob, who lives in Wilmington, North Carolina, offered to transport the dog back to his vet, in preparation for Nathan's imminent move to Columbia, South Carolina. "We decided I would take him on my boat back to West Palm Beach and then drive from there," says Rob. "If we

Dingo with Rob Moody, who helped bring Dingo to the United States

had been stopped by border patrol with no records for a dog, we wouldn't have made it."

After a 12-hour car ride, Dingo arrived in Wilmington, where he would spend weeks in the care of vet Dr. Michele Rohrer while she fought to save his foot. "Dingo is happy, kind, and sweet," says Rohrer, "and he has a will to live." No one feels more strongly about Dingo than Nathan, in whom Dingo has found another beloved companion. "There is so much strength in his eyes, so much personality," says Nathan. "He went through so much trauma, and is such a fighter. There's just something about him. I've fallen in love." ◆

JUST HOW AMAZING IS DINGO'S SURVIVAL? Dogs need water every day, as 70 percent of their body is made up of water. Dogs will die if their body loses even one-tenth of its water. To survive, an average medium-size dog requires at least two ounces of water every day.

Wilma

PIT BULL ◆ NEW YORK

Thanks to Wilma, Steve Sietos may very well be the world's only fireman/herbalist/energy healer. He certainly is the only one in his Brooklyn, New York, engine company. He was a recent Fire Academy graduate when his captain appeared with a dog he had found. At about six months old, Wilma was hungry, her hair was matted, her tongue hung out of her mouth at an odd angle, and she had a badly torn-up paw. But she never stopped wagging her tail. "We threw her in the rig and brought her to the vet," he says, "where they told us she had an infection and stitched her up. The captain said, 'Who wants this dog?' and I knew I did—it was like I knew her—but I was a junior guy and you don't speak unless you're spoken to."

For one week a different fireman took the pit bull home each night, only to return her, saying they couldn't keep her, even though they all agreed that she was the sweetest dog they had ever met. The problem was that she self-mutilated, ripping the pads off the bottoms of her paws until they bled. In a last-ditch effort, the captain brought Wilma back to the vet, who suggested she be put to sleep.

THE NEW YORK Fire Department's mascot is a Dalmatian named Hotdog, who teaches children and families about fire safety.

OPPOSITE: *Wilma was rescued by the captain of Steve Sietos's firehouse; Sietos later adopted her.*

FIREHOUSE DOGS

- The Dalmatian has been the iconic firehouse dog, dating back 200 years.
- Today, firehouse dogs mostly serve as guard dogs, mascots, and companions to firefighters.
- In 2012, the National Fire Dog Monument went on a 2,000-mile cross-country tour before being erected outside a Washington, D.C., firehouse.

"That's when I knew I could speak up," remembers Sietos.

Wilma was diagnosed with cerebral palsy—she couldn't walk more than a block without collapsing—but her physical suffering didn't seem to affect her spirit. "She is sweet and shy, like me," says Sietos. "And I don't know how to explain it, but she has such an energy about her. I knew she didn't want to die. " But $8,000 in vet bills later, Wilma was no better, and Sietos was bankrupt, walking to work because he couldn't afford to take the subway. In desperation, he called a psychic suggested by a friend.

"She said, 'Oh, honey, your angels are coming in and there's nothing you can do, you'll have to put her down. I will pray for you both,'" Sietos remembers. "I cried for about five days straight, and Wilma was licking my eyes the whole time and that's when I said to myself, 'No more vets.' So I started researching herbs and flower essences online that help immune systems, and that was the beginning of her healing." It was also the beginning of Sietos's path to becoming a clinical herbalist, now helping people as well as dogs in need.

Sietos changed Wilma's diet as alternative medicine dictates for people with compromised immune systems: no carbohydrates, no yeast. He also began giving her a daily regimen of herbs. Soon, he was planning regimens for friends who were ill, as well. He says that his colleagues were bemused if grudgingly tolerant, teasing him that he was a "witch doctor," until he helped a colleague's wife who was struggling with chemotherapy. Thanks to that, as well as the tinctures for muscle aches and the holistic cold remedies that he leaves in the firehouse kitchen, Sietos says his colleagues have embraced his other

Sietos performs an energetic cleansing by lighting salt—a purification element—on fire like a candle.

career as a clinical herbalist and healer. "I'm treating the guys at the firehouse and their friends and their families," he says. "They have been the best trainers because they can be a rough crowd," with a definite soft side for a certain pit bull. Wilma is welcome at the firehouse and accompanies Sietos when he works a 24-hour shift.

The only sign of Wilma's difficult path is that she wears makeshift "shoes" to protect her feet, which Sietos treats with herbal poultices, and although her tongue still hangs out at a funny angle, "she's so beautiful," says Sietos. "She's not perfect, but no one is. She's been the best teacher I've ever had. She's my main squeeze." ◆

HISTORY OF THE FIREFIGHTER'S BEST FRIEND Dogs have been a part of firehouses for more than 200 years. Fire departments depended on horse-drawn firefighting equipment, and dogs proved useful in keeping the horses calm. They would also be used to guard the stables and rid the firehouse of rodents.

Santina

MIXED BREED ♦ KENTUCKY

I n January 1988, artist Mark Barone was walking to his church in Paducah, Kentucky, where he volunteered as a youth minister, when he passed an abandoned, boarded-up apartment building with a small German shepherd mixed breed sitting on the stoop. As he approached to pet her, the dog began to yelp in fear, so Barone continued on his way. But as he walked past her again on his way home, the dog followed. ◆ After they had played together on his lawn for a while, Barone went inside, assuming the dog would go back home. Two hours later, with the temperature now hovering in the teens, the dog was still there, lying on the welcome mat. "I called my wife at the time and said, 'What do I do?'" Barone remembers. "And she said, 'Bring her in.' And that was how we got Santina."

Santina's favorite place was by her master's side. "She was around me 24/7," says Barone. Santina and Rudy, a dog he adopted later, "were my stability and my foundation." But a decade after Santina arrived, Barone's marriage had ended in divorce, and he was drinking to excess. One night, as he sat drinking in a largely unfurnished house—"The one thing I asked for and got

THE VARIOUS
PRESIDENTS
of the United States
have owned 118 dogs
while they have been
in office.

OPPOSITE: *Santina, pictured at the age of 21, inspired his owner to help rescue dogs across America.*

A sample of some of the portraits Mark Barone has painted of dogs euthanized in American shelters.

was my dogs"—he looked at the dogs and was gripped with fear, and then clarity. "Here they were, completely dependent on me, and I couldn't take care of myself. How could I take care of them?" Barone remembers. "I got up and poured out all the liquor in the house. The next morning, I went to my first AA meeting."

Santina, along with Rudy, became a vital part of Barone's recovery. "I would get up at 5 a.m. because they wanted to walk, and that became a walking meditation for me," he says. "Without them, I would have been left to nothing but my own thinking, and my own thinking was so screwed up at that point."

In July 2010, at the age of 21, Santina died. "I was depressed for at least six months," says Barone, who is now living with his partner,

- Pablo Picasso and Andy Warhol both owned dachshunds. Picasso's dog was named Lump, and Warhol's were Archie and Amos.
- Georgia O'Keeffe raised six chow chows during her life.
- René Magritte and his wife raised canaries and a Pomeranian, Loulou.

Marina Dervan. "Before her, I had never experienced the love of a dog," says Dervan. "She changed my life."

The couple could never have guessed how much. When Dervan began to research shelters online to find a new dog to adopt, she learned about the country's euthanasia rate for unwanted pets. She told Barone they had to do something to educate people. The next morning, he presented a plan: He would paint 5,500 portraits—an approximation of the number of dogs euthanized each day in the United States—of those who hadn't made it. They dubbed the project An Act of Dog.

While Barone works from pictures provided by rescue sites, Dervan, with their new hound-boxer mix, Gigi, by her side, is searching for a philanthropist or city to partner with to help house this memorial-museum. The Act of Dog Foundation aims to raise $20 million for organizations that have committed to making the transition to no-kill by adopting the No-Kill Equation—programs and services adopted and implemented by organizations that take steps to end euthanasia of animals—and to all other solution-oriented groups aiming to make American a no-kill nation.

"If Santina hadn't followed me home, this never would have happened," says Barone. "What she did for me in my life was so profound. She allowed me to find my calling." ◆

POKER FACE "Dogs Playing Poker" is one in a series of 16 oil paintings of dogs in human situations by Cassius Marcellus Coolidge, originally created for the advertising firm Brown and Bigelow in 1903. In 2005, two of the original paintings were sold for $590,400.

Resources

COMPANIONS FOR HEROES

www.companionsforheroes.org
1-866-701-7553
INFO@companionsforheroes.org

SURFICE DOG INITIATIVE

www.puppyprodigies.org
707-228-0679
PuppyProdigies@aol.com

ROSE BROOKS CENTER

www.rosebrooks.org

EDUCATED CANINES ASSISTING WITH DISABILITIES

www.ecad1.org
914-693-000 ext. 1950 or 1953
info@ecad1.org

COURTHOUSE DOGS

www.courthousedogs.com
celeste@courthousedogs.org

NUNEATON AND WARWICKSHIRE WILDLIFE SANCTUARY

www.nuneatonwildlife.co.uk
+44 (0)2476 345243
info@nuneatonwildlife.co.uk

DOBERMAN ASSISTANCE NETWORK

www.dobermanassistance.org
danboard@dobermanassistance.org

PILOTS N PAWS

www.pilotsnpaws.org
info@pilotsnpaws.org

BRUISED NOT BROKEN

www.bruisednotbroken.com
dave@bruisednotbroken.com

NATIONAL DISASTER SEARCH DOG FOUNDATION

www.searchdogfoundation.org
(888) 459-4376
Rescue@SearchDogFoundation.org

WHEELS OF PROGRESS

www.wheelsofprogress.org
(347) 645-3265

DOGS FOR THE DEAF

www.dogsforthedeaf.org
1-800-990-DOGS
info@dogsforthedeaf.org

CLOSE TO HOME ANIMAL RESCUE

www.cthar.org

PUPS ON PAROLE

www.lassenhumanesociety.com/pop.html
(530) 257-4555
lassenhumanesociety@yahoo.com

LILLY'S FUND

www.lillytheheropitbull.com
LillytheHeroPitbull@hotmail.com

AN ACT OF DOG

www.anactofdog.org
270-519-0967
info@anactofdog.org

Illustrations Credits

Cover, David duChemin; 2, Brad DeCecco; 6, Ellen Watson; 8, The *Washington Post*/Getty Images; 11, The *Washington Post*/Getty Images; 12, The *Washington Post*/Getty Images; 15, Splash News/Newscom; 16, AP Photo/Lenny Ignelzi; 18, Brooke Lim; 20, Tao Chin Lim; 22, Hannah Stonehouse Hudson; 25, Hannah Stonehouse Hudson; 26, Linda Murphy; 30, Jay Town/AFP/Getty Images; 31, Jim Smith/AFP/Getty Images; 32, Photograph by Dale E. Smith, Courtesy Paw Prints the Magazine; 35, David A. Riffel; 36, Sharon Cantillon/The *Buffalo News;* 39, Topps trading cards used courtesy of the Topps Company, Inc. For more information about the Topps Company, please see our website at www.topps.com; 40, Kelly Shimoda/the *N.Y. Times*/Redux Pictures; 43, Dale Picard; 44, Lu Picard; 46, Caters News/ZUMA Press/Newscom; 49, Caters News/ZUMA Press/Newscom; 50, Elaine Heath; 53, Elaine Heath; 54, Richard Olsenius/National Geographic Stock; 59, Deborah L. Boies, co-founder Pilots N Paws; 60, Bill Simmons; 63, Bill Simmons; 64, Dan

Devoted

38 Extraordinary Tales of Love, Loyalty, and Life With Dogs

Rebecca Ascher-Walsh

Prepared by the Book Division

Hector Sierra, *Senior Vice President and General Manager*
Janet Goldstein, *Senior Vice President and Editorial Director*
Jonathan Halling, *Design Director, Books and Children's Publishing*
Marianne R. Koszorus, *Design Director, Books*
R. Gary Colbert, *Production Director*
Jennifer A. Thornton, *Director of Managing Editorial*
Susan S. Blair, *Director of Photography*
Meredith C. Wilcox, *Director, Administration and Rights Clearance*

Staff for This Book

Bridget A. English, *Editor*
Melissa Farris, *Art Director*
Meredith Wilcox, *Illustrations Editor*
Michelle Harris, *Researcher*
Marshall Kiker, *Associate Managing Editor*
Judith Klein, *Production Editor*
Michael Horenstein, *Production Manager*
Katie Olsen, *Production Design Assistant*
Anne Smyth, *Assistant Editor*

Manufacturing and Quality Management

Phillip L. Schlosser, *Senior Vice President*
Chris Brown, *Vice President, NG Book Manufacturing*
George Bounelis, *Vice President, Production Services*
Nicole Elliott, *Manager*
Rachel Faulise, *Manager*
Robert L. Barr, *Manager*

Since 1888, the National Geographic Society has funded more than 14,000 research, conservation, education, and storytelling projects around the world. National Geographic Partners distributes a portion of the funds it receives from your purchase to National Geographic Society to support programs including the conservation of animals and their habitats.

National Geographic Partners, LLC
1145 17th Street NW
Washington, DC 20036-4688 USA

Get closer to National Geographic explorers and photographers, and connect with our global community. Join us today at nationalgeographic.org/joinus

For rights or permissions inquiries, please contact National Geographic Books Subsidiary Rights: bookrights@natgeo.com

ISBN: 978-1-4262-1158-4

Printed in China

22/PPS/6